101 Great Games for
Infants, Toddlers
& Preschoolers

101 Great Games for

Games for

Infants, Toddlers
& Preschoolers

Active, Bible-Based Fun
for Christian Education

Jolene L.
Roehlkepartain

Abingdon Press

Nashville

101 GREAT GAMES FOR INFANTS, TODDLERS & PRESCHOOLERS
ACTIVE, BIBLE-BASED FUN FOR CHRISTIAN EDUCATION

Copyright © 2004 by Abingdon Press

This book is printed on acid-free paper.

Library of Congress Cataloging-in-Publication Data

Roehlkepartain, Jolene L., 1962-
  101 great games for infants, toddlers and preschoolers : active, Bible-based fun for Christian education / Jolene L. Roehlkepartain.
    p. cm.
  Includes bibliograpical references and indexes.
  ISBN 0-687-00814-X (binding: adhesive, pbk. : alk. paper)
  1. Games in Christian education. 2. Church work with children. I. Title: One hundred one great games for infants, toddlers and preschoolers. II. Title: One hundred and one great games for infants, toddlers and preschoolers. III. Title.

BV1536.3.R63 2004
268'.432—dc22

2004012954

Scripture quotations noted NIV are taken from the HOLY BIBLE: NEW INTERNATIONAL VERSION. Copyright © 1973, 1978, 1984 by the International Bible Society. Used by permission of Zondervan Publishing House. All rights reserved.

Scripture quotations marked (GNT) are from the Good News Translation in Today's English Version-Second Edition. Copyright © 1992 by American Bible Society. Used by permission.

04 05 06 07 08 09 10 11 12 13—10 9 8 7 6 5 4 3 2 1

MANUFACTURED IN THE UNITED STATES OF AMERICA

To Merry Obrecht Sawdey,
who delights in the wonders and magic
of young children

Contents

Introduction
The Power of Play

Volunteers in one church nursery play games with infants and toddlers in addition to caring for their needs. Volunteers know that they're nurturing the faith life of babies and toddlers—even though many of these young children only gurgle, grunt, and coo.

* * *

Whenever a toddler or preschooler starts to squirm or whine during a worship service, an elderly member of the church pulls a rag doll out of her purse and passes it to the child. This former teacher makes these dolls and keeps a stash in her purse to help children deal with their natural wiggles.

* * *

A group of adults in another congregation noticed that the exhausted parents of a colicky baby spent more time leaving worship than staying. These adults took turns comforting and playing with the infant so that the parents could enjoy the chance to worship.

* * *

Learning Through Play

Play. That's the way infants, toddlers, and preschoolers explore themselves, their world—and their faith. Playing lays the foundation for young children to learn about love, faith, scripture, and caring. Researchers claim that young children's play is a serious activity,[1] and when we take their playtimes seriously, we help young children grow spiritually.

What young children get out of play is often radically different from what adults perceive they absorb. From an adult's viewpoint, so much of young children's play seems pointless and does not make much sense. Young children wander from one activity to another. They often create huge messes, and their emotions can overwhelm them. Yet young children explore and expand their world through dawdling and dallying.

Too often while some church leaders wait until children are older to introduce children to God's world, these same young children are becoming well-versed in Elmo's world—or even scarier worlds that the media can bring them. Young children in our society know more about Big Bird, Mickey Mouse, and Barney than they do about God and Jesus. "Our hope is that the child will—over time—affirm that this is *my* story about *me*, and it is *our* story about *us*," writes scripture scholar Walter Brueggemann.[2] The key is that this takes time, and the sooner we start, the quicker we'll have a positive influence on young children's spiritual development.

What if we started teaching children about the Bible from day one? What if infants had picture Bibles to play with in addition to rattles? What if toddlers could easily name Jesus when you pointed to pictures of him? What if your preschoolers talked about lions in the Bible and how God kept people safe when they visited the zoo?

"We can embark on a spiritual journey with children, teaching them and learning from them along the way," writes Karen Marie Yust in *Real Kids, Real Faith: Practices for Nurturing Children's Spiritual Lives*.[3] Infants and toddlers can surprise us and teach us as much as preschoolers can. Young children have a way of showing busy adults how to slow down and marvel at the fact that "apples are red, and water is wet."

Nurturing Children's Faith

How do you nurture children's faith? When do you begin? Educators, volunteers, and parents ask these two questions over and over, and new resources continually guide us in identifying effective ways to develop our children's spirituality. Research suggests beginning as soon as children are born (or technically when a child is conceived by nurturing the faith of the expectant parents). "We all begin the pilgrimage of faith as infants," writes researcher James Fowler.[4]

Nurturing children's faith happens primarily through interactions. "The core of Christianity is relationship," writes researcher Cynthia Dixon. "It is about belonging to God and one another."[5] Newborns learn how much they are loved and valued by how caregivers interact with them in the church nursery and how members of a congregation react when they see and hear these young children. Even as children grow and develop, relationships are key.[6]

Without significant relationships, young children will not bond to a congregation or to their natural spirit within them. As children get older, they'll resist going to church. Although many cite boredom the truth is that they do not feel they belong. When congregations are loving, warm, and open to young children, when they delight in the unique contributions children make, young children will feel valued. They'll know the church is their church.

Embracing children in the church entails journeying with them through the ups and downs of faith. Young children can say profound statements of faith, such as "I just love God for making lots of flowers," and they also often miss the point, which we adults don't like to admit. One preschooler dominated a game about Noah's ark by telling everyone how the motor fell off his dad's boat in the lake, loudly repeating the curses his dad said. To a young child, the concrete is more vivid than the abstract. Children will walk away with their ideas about a Bible story based on their personal experience.

That's why researcher James Fowler urges caregivers, educators, and parents to create an atmosphere where the child "can freely express, verbally and nonverbally, the images she or he is forming."[7] Allowing this openness is delightful when young children articulate simple tenets of the faith, but it also can be frightening when they not only misunderstand but also pull an entire group in the wrong direction. Fowler says the way young children learn is unpredictable, even under the best teachers.[8] This is due to the way young children develop, not the way they are taught. Fowler recommends teaching children in ways that are "life opening and sustaining of love, faith, and courage."[9] Sometimes when everything in a game or lesson goes wrong, your strong display of love and warmth will be the teaching point that young children remember.

Teaching Through Play

Although young children will occasionally misunderstand a game or teaching point, it's important for adults to surround young children with the stories of faith. Abstract beliefs, theological concepts, and complex symbols may make up the Christian faith, but young children still can learn about the Bible and their faith through play. In one congregation, a teacher created a church box that included a number of spiritual objects for the three- and four-year-olds to play with. Each week during the class for young preschoolers, the three- and four-year-olds anxiously waited to see which new items would appear. Sometimes the objects were ordinary, such as a rock or a leaf. Other times, they were magical, such as a large heart made out of red glitter that sparkled as children played with it.

When children play with spiritual objects, they get to know those objects. The cross that hangs in the church no longer seems so distant when young children have a cross to cradle. They're more enthusiastic about putting something in the offering plate when they play with offering plates and envelopes. Once objects of faith become familiar to them, they sometimes even use them in their imaginary play. In one congregation during free playtime, a couple of children created a church of stuffed animals. The stuffed dog was the minister, and the bunnies passed around bowls to other stuffed animals who deposited play money into the offering plates. This type of imaginary play only emerges when educators, volunteers, and parents immerse young children in the rituals of daily faith.

The more young children become part of the life of the church and experience the stories of faith, the more they'll spontaneously create play that illustrates this part of their lives. Spiritual objects to consider for playtime (or a church box or a God learning table) may include:

- A cross
- A children's Bible
- A red, stuffed heart
- A large illustration of Jesus
- A box of offering envelopes
- Animals in pairs
- A picture Bible
- A miniature manger or nativity set
- Bread and juice play food (to role-play communion)
- Other toys[10]

You may even want to encourage children to dress up in outfits that church leaders and members wear. Make different-colored stoles out of felt. Collect plain superhero capes to use as choir robes (or see if your church has any old children's robes). Identify other dress-up clothes children can use to reenact Bible stories. Some congregations even have old costumes from prior children's pageants, such as shepherd and sheep costumes.

If you have carpenters in your congregation, consider asking them to construct a play church the size of a dollhouse.[11] Young children love playing with dollhouses, and few get the opportunity to play with a wooden dollhouse, let alone a church dollhouse. Imagine a church dollhouse that not only includes the sanctuary but also the fellowship hall and the nursery. Imagine what young children would say—and play.

It is critical to give young children the chance to use and play with spiritual objects. This includes Bibles. I often like to have a number of different picture Bibles placed strategically around the room. I tuck one in the book corner and place another on the floor with the hope that an infant will stop and take a look. I usually keep one Bible to show children that the games we're playing come from stories in the Bible. (See "Best Bibles for Young Children" on page 157 for different picture Bibles to use with infants, toddlers, and preschoolers.) In one congregation, church leaders present each two-year-old with a toddler picture Bible. The toddlers page through the colorful pictures with glee, and parents learn that it's not too early to read simple Bible stories to their children.

"Spiritual nurture is not a process of staging extraordinary experiences for our children, but one of enabling them to become more aware of their spiritual connection that is as natural to them as breathing," says author Jean Grasso Fitzpatrick.[12] "If we nurture a child's spirituality from an early age, we can trust that it will one day find expression and maturity in adult terms."[13]

Using the Games in This Book

This book provides 101 Bible games for young children. You'll find twenty games designed for infants (up to twelve months old), twenty games for young toddlers (one- to two-year-olds), twenty games for older toddlers (two- to three-year-olds), twenty games for young preschoolers (three- to four-year-olds), and twenty-one games for older preschoolers (four- to five-year-olds). Each game includes a scripture passage, a teaching point, a supervision tip, materials needed, and game instructions. Some games require little preparation and no materials. Others involve more effort. A number of games also include a bonus idea or a bonus tip for how to play the game in a different way. A scripture index on page 163 and a topical index on page 165 provide information on locating games that tie into specific scriptures and teaching points. Half of the games in this book feature Old Testament stories and teachings; the other half relate to the New Testament.

Young children have a lot of energy, and they learn best when they can move and play. By using these games, you can help young children:

- have fun
- play in new ways
- work with their wiggles instead of against them
- learn about key Bible messages and stories

Even as babies are beginning to crawl, toddlers are learning to speak, and preschoolers are starting to cooperate with playmates, they can begin to discover God's word and God's world through play. These 101 new games give young children the foundation they need in ways that are fun and exciting.

When you play with young children, follow their lead. Let them initiate nine out of ten games that you play together. (Use the games in this book for the games you suggest.) As you play, "follow the giggles," recommends author Lawrence J. Cohen.[14] Repeat what makes young children laugh and gets them excited. When their interest begins to wane, drop the activity and see what the child wants to do next.

Embracing the Delights of Each Age

Playing with a four-year-old is radically different from playing with a seven-month-old. Researchers and child development experts have created overviews of each age group and recommended ways to interact with them. The section "Best Resources on Early Childhood Development" on page 161 recommends resources that explore how children grow and change at each age.

The more you know about how children think, move, interact, and express themselves emotionally and spiritually, the more fun you will have—and the more children will soak up key concepts.

Understanding Infants (Ages Birth to 12 Months)

The Mind (Intellectual Development)

- Infants learn mainly through their mouths and hands. Their sucking and grasping give them a lot of information about their world.
- They reach for nearby objects and toys, which stimulate their thinking.
- They have a very short attention span and move quickly from one object or activity to the next.
- They explore objects by banging, dropping, shaking, throwing, or sucking on them.
- Ordinary household items (such as egg cartons and plastic cups) fascinate and stimulate infants.
- By the end of seven months, most infants can find objects that are partially hidden.

The Body (Physical Development)

• The first year of physical growth for infants is rapid. They go from using mainly their eyes and mouths (as newborns) to using their whole bodies to explore, move around, and embrace the world.

• By three months, most infants can raise their head and chest when placed on their stomach, open and shut their hands, bring their hands to their mouth, and grasp for toys with both hands.

• By seven months, many infants can sit up, roll over (from back to front and from front to back), grasp for toys with one hand, and move objects and toys from one hand to another.

• By twelve months, most infants can crawl (or creep or scoot) and pull themselves to stand, and they may stand momentarily without support and walk by hanging onto furniture or other stationary, heavy objects.

The Emotions (Emotional Development)

• For the first three months of their lives, infants are focused on getting their needs met—getting enough food, sleep, affection, and comfort. Their emotional state depends on their comfort.

• They respond to people's facial expressions and emotions.

• They may cry after playing stops to show that they want to play more.

• Some infants are more emotionally sensitive than others are and may prefer different levels of light, sound, and stimulation.

The Spirit (Spiritual Development)

• When infants are positively cared for consistently and in response to their needs, they're more apt to develop a sense of basic trust, which lays the foundation for their spirit to develop in positive ways.

• Infants who are loved by trustworthy adults learn that the world and God are worth exploring and embracing.

• Although researchers find it difficult to measure and identify the spiritual development of infants, they do see strong correlations between the way an infant is cared for and later spiritual development. Infants who have their needs met and are loved are more likely to have the seeds of trust, hope, and love planted in them. Those who are deprived in some ways and experience a number of

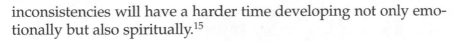

inconsistencies will have a harder time developing not only emotionally but also spiritually.[15]

Understanding Young Toddlers (Ages 1 to 2 Years)

The Mind (Intellectual Development)

• A lot of learning occurs through imitation. Young toddlers will observe you closely and try to do some of the actions you do, such as comb your hair and talk on the phone.

• They understand more of how things work but do not grasp consequences. For example, young toddlers know that doors open and close, but they often get their fingers slammed in the door because they do not have the cognitive ability to keep their fingers away.

• Between fifteen and eighteen months, most young toddlers can speak a number of single words. By twenty-four months, most use simple phrases and two- to four-word sentences.

• By the age of two, many start imaginary play.

• They constantly ask "what?" to learn names of objects, places, and people.

The Body (Physical Development)

• They'll spend most of the year practicing their walk until it becomes steadier.

• Most young toddlers often trip and fall because of their wobbly sense of balance.

• As they get close to two years and develop more gross-motor skills, they'll begin to run, climb (particularly on furniture), and kick things.

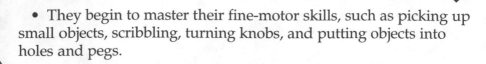

- They begin to master their fine-motor skills, such as picking up small objects, scribbling, turning knobs, and putting objects into holes and pegs.

The Emotions (Emotional Development)

- Young toddlers have extreme emotions. They swing between pushing adults away and clinging to them.
- They can throw violent tantrums, kicking, pushing, and knocking things over.
- When they're tired, sick, or upset, they stick close to adults in search of comfort.
- Young toddlers are impulsive at this age, rushing into what excites them, whether it's for a new toy or out into the middle of traffic.
- Many young toddlers still cry a lot.

The Spirit (Spiritual Development)

- Young toddlers assume that what they experience is the only way to experience God (even though they are too young to articulate this). For example, a young toddler who is loved, given appropriate limits, and exposed to stimulating activity often later assumes that God is good and loving. A young toddler who often is threatened, chastised, and hurt by adults (either emotionally or physically) typically will later see God as mean and inaccessible.
- Actions teach young toddlers more than words. If an adult hugs them and says that God loves them, they will understand that more than if an adult only says so.
- Exposing young toddlers to the language of faith (even the abstract concepts) helps young children see that faith is part of growing up.[16]

Understanding Older Toddlers (Ages 2 to 3 Years)

The Mind (Intellectual Development)

- Children between the ages of twenty-four and thirty months may seem to have even shorter attention spans than young toddlers and infants. This has to do with some rather large leaps in the development of their minds during this period, which makes it hard for them to concentrate.

• The learning process for older toddlers (between thirty and thirty-six months) becomes more thoughtful, and they can begin to understand some simple abstract thoughts. For example, older toddlers can understand that "we will have a snack after we wash our hands" without needing to see the snack or the sink.

• They enjoy imaginary play with animals, people, and dolls. Some children also will do imaginary play with trucks and miniature playhouses and towns.

• They comprehend a sense of space, mainly in regard to opposites: outside and inside, up and down, and high and low.

The Body (Physical Development)

• Older toddlers are constantly on the go. They run, kick, climb, jump, and throw. Some seem to tackle the world.

• They begin to practice and master new movements, such as walking backward, standing on one leg, and walking up and down steps while holding onto a railing.

• Their hand and finger skills become more refined. Older toddlers can turn pages of a book, one page at a time, and can hold a crayon more erect for coloring.

• Instead of pulling objects, they enjoy pushing them, such as wagons and strollers.

• During this period, their sense of balance becomes better so that by the time they turn three, most young children can bend over without falling.

The Emotions (Emotional Development)

• Conflicts become even more frequent, since children at this age have a hard time making decisions. If you give them two choices (like you did when they were younger), they will choose one and then immediately the other, becoming upset about not being able to choose both.

• They are heavily into the my-and-mine stage where they refuse to share and often do not like to interact with other children.

• They have intense mood swings: exuberant one moment and inconsolable the next.

• Despite their strong emotional displays, children at this age need a lot of assurances and reassurances.

• When they're exhausted, they whine and may refuse to nap because so many activities capture their attention.

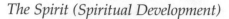

The Spirit (Spiritual Development)

• Older toddlers are more likely to see how spiritual development is as important as other parts of their development if simple faith rituals show up in their daily lives, such as praying before meals and bedtime, attending worship on a regular basis, and reading the Bible (such as a picture Bible).

• Even though they are too young to understand most theological and biblical concepts, they pick up on the emotional climate in which these concepts are taught. Older toddlers who are with loving, playful adults at church will find spiritual development more appealing.

• The spiritual development of older toddlers often mimics the behavior of adults around them. Older toddlers will scream and yell more often when they're around screaming adults, but if they see that adults are giving and loving, they will be more apt to act that way, too.

Understanding Young Preschoolers (Ages 3 to 4 Years)

The Mind (Intellectual Development)

• Young preschoolers are very aware of their daily routine and which activities follow other activities.

• They begin to understand similarities and differences in people, objects, and places.

• They constantly ask "why."

• By age three, they tend to have a vocabulary of at least three hundred words and can speak in five- to six-word sentences. By age four, they'll know at least fifteen hundred words.

• They can follow three-part commands. For example, "Let's dry our hands, sit down at the table, and color."

• They begin to recognize some colors.

The Body (Physical Development)

• Most young preschoolers have mastered walking, running, riding a tricycle, and standing. They concentrate their efforts more on hopping, tiptoeing, and catching a ball, which are challenging.

• They continue to get a lot of bumps and bruises while they constantly test what they can (and cannot do) physically. Most children at this age become uncoordinated (and may seem more so than older toddlers) because they are learning new physical skills that send them off balance.

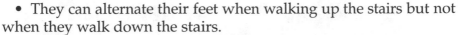

- They can alternate their feet when walking up the stairs but not when they walk down the stairs.
- They become more adept at assembling puzzles (putting together four or five large-piece puzzles), stringing large wooden beads, and undressing dolls. (They tend to be more interested in undressing dolls than dressing them.)
- They begin to use scissors (although their use is rather rudimentary), and they begin to draw circles and squares. Some even begin to copy capital letters and simple numbers.

The Emotions (Emotional Development)

- Around the age of three and a half, many young preschoolers develop an insecurity. Instead of holding onto a railing to walk up the stairs, they want to hold the hand of an adult instead. They're often more interested in being with adults rather than exploring the world away from adults.
- They're very attached to their parents, and they often play "Mom" or "Dad" during imaginary play times.
- They may develop fears, such as fear of the dark, fear of monsters, and fear of thunder. Work with their fears. If they're afraid they'll fall when they walk down the stairs, hold their hands.
- They cannot tell the difference between fantasy and reality, which is why adults need to keep them from seeing violent cartoons and news programs that show violence.
- They may become resistant in the middle of an activity. If that happens, change the activity so that you don't get locked into a power struggle.

The Spirit (Spiritual Development)

- Young preschoolers are old enough to understand that praying is a way to talk to God.
- They enjoy helping others and doing service projects.
- They make connections between the way adults treat them and the way they think God would treat them. If adults are nice, loving, and helpful, they're more apt to assume that God is that way, too.
- If they're often brought to church and are raised in an environment where adults often talk about God and religious issues, they often begin to ask questions about God at this age.

Understanding Older Preschoolers (Ages 4 to 5 Years)

The Mind (Intellectual Development)

- They learn mainly through experience and the five senses.
- They can usually identify at least four colors and can often count to ten.
- Language bursts from about fifteen hundred words (at age four) to about five thousand words (at age five).
- They're curious and enjoy learning (if that has been and continues to be nurtured by adults).
- They know how everyday items work: they know that water comes out of a faucet, that money is used to buy things, that a washing machine cleans their clothes, and that a car or bus takes them places.
- They learn the correct labels for shapes.
- They have an active imagination and enjoy fantasy play.

The Body (Physical Development)

- Older preschoolers (particularly those who enjoy physical activity) will enjoy hopping, somersaulting, standing on one foot for at least twenty seconds, and maybe even skipping.
- Their hand and finger skills are more developed. Many can cut fairly well, draw a person with a body, print some alphabet letters, and trace somewhat complex shapes, such as diamonds and stars.
- By age five, a preschooler has balance and coordination that is almost equal to an adult.
- They have boundless energy, and most enjoy a lot of physical activity.
- Children at this age need a lot of room, not only for movement but also for projects.

The Emotions (Emotional Development)

- Emotional expression becomes more distinct and related to personality. Some older preschoolers are emotionally expressive; others struggle to show their feelings. A lot of adult coaching can help children at this age grow emotionally.
- Children at this age begin to distinguish between fantasy and reality, although this understanding won't be complete until around age seven.

- Many children become aware of sexuality at this age and may ask questions about where babies come from and how the bodies of boys and girls are different.
- Their imaginary play often includes violent themes. This does not mean children are violent, but it is their way developmentally of figuring out the difference between good and bad, right and wrong.
- They have strong feelings toward certain peers. Often friendships begin to develop at this age.

The Spirit (Spiritual Development)

- Older preschoolers pick up more on adults' emotions toward God and spirituality than on what adults say. Not only do they witness adult emotions, they also can sense when an adult is hiding an emotion.
- They make assumptions about God and spirituality based on personal experience. If they have positive, joyful experiences at church, they believe that God is a positive, joyful God.
- They can begin to say simple prayers and participate in simple religious rituals, such as placing money in the offering plate, singing simple songs (such as "Jesus Loves Me"), and helping others.
- They can learn simple theological concepts, such as God exists, God loves you, Jesus loves you, the Bible tells stories about God, we are part of a Christian family, our Christian family worships God together, God is with us wherever we go, and God created everything. When theological concepts are taught in concrete, experiential ways, older preschoolers will likely have the spirit within them awaken and develop.

Notes

1. Burton L. White, *The First Three Years of Life: New and Revised* (New York: Prentice Hall Press, 1985, 1990), 276.

2. Walter Brueggemann, *Belonging and Growing in the Christian Community* (Crawfordsville, Ind.: General Assembly Mission Board, Presbyterian Church in the United States, 1979), 31.

3. Karen Marie Yust, *Real Kids, Real Faith: Practices for Nurturing Children's Spiritual Lives* (San Francisco: Jossey-Bass, 2004).

4. James W. Fowler, *Stages of Faith: The Psychology of Human Development and the Quest for Meaning* (San Francisco: HarperSanFrancisco, 1981), 119.

5. Cynthia Dixon, "Who Nurtured the Child? Without Attachment There Can Be No Intimacy," in *Spiritual Education: Cultural, Religious, and Social*

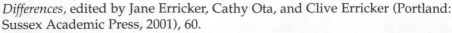

Differences, edited by Jane Erricker, Cathy Ota, and Clive Erricker (Portland: Sussex Academic Press, 2001), 60.

6. Children, Youth, and Family Consortium, "Researchers Agree on What Kids Need to Succeed," in *Seeds of Promise* volume 1, number 1 (St. Paul: University of Minnesota, April 1996), 2, 5.

7. Fowler, *Stages of Faith*, 133.

8. Ibid., 132.

9. Ibid.

10. Christian toys aren't always easy to find for young children. Fisher-Price currently sells a Little People® Noah's Ark designed for one- to five-year-olds along with additional animals with Little People® Hippos, Pandas, and Alligators and Little People® Peacocks, Leopards, and Rhinos. This set is ideal since it's plastic and is easily washable. Tiny Love offers the Tiny Love Gymini Delux: Noah's Ark Design, an activity mat for babies, which features animals from Noah's Ark. Pockets of Learning has the SS Noah Soft Sculpture with moveable animals. Unfortunately, most Christian toys emphasize only the Noah's Ark story, and manufacturers tend to discontinue them once sales drop off.

11. Hobby Builders Supply of Doraville, Georgia (800-926-6464; www.miniatures.com) sells a country church dollhouse kit that includes stained-glass windows, a steeple, pews, an altar, and a pulpit.

12. Jean Grasso Fitzpatrick, *Something More: Nurturing Your Child's Spiritual Growth* (New York: Viking, 1991), 48-49.

13. Ibid., 25.

14. Lawrence J. Cohen, *Playful Parenting: A Bold New Way to Nurture Close Connections, Solve Behavior Problems, and Encourage Children's Confidence* (New York: Ballantine, 2002), 76-92.

15. Fowler, *Stages of Faith*, 119-21.

16. Yust, *Real Kids, Real Faith*.

Fun Games for
INFANTS
(FROM BIRTH TO 12 MONTHS)

Playing with an infant always starts with the infant. Even though there are countless games that adults can initiate with babies (and many are enjoyable for both infants and adults), let the infant take the lead. How? By monitoring closely what the infant wants. If a baby wants to sleep, follow that. If an infant gurgles and grasps for your nose, take that as an invitation to play. Begin by following the infant's lead, such as when a baby discovers and shakes a rattle or crawls across the floor to get a certain toy. Usually what infants want (more than anything) is the chance to play with an adult.

The games in this section have been designed to start giving the infant the idea that spirituality is fun and something worth exploring. Although infants will not understand the point of the game, they will experience whether it's fun, whether the interaction they're having with the adult is enjoyable, and whether the game is worth repeating.

When playing with infants, remember that their care always comes first. If you're in the middle of the game and the baby begins to fuss, stop immediately and determine why the infant is upset. If the child is hungry, feed him or her. Change a diaper if needed. Or if the baby just wants some snuggling time, do that. Since the spiritual development of infants is so closely tied to how their needs are met, their care is your top priority.

Of course, infants need interesting stimulation and important one-on-one time with adults. Playing is essential. Play helps cement the bond between an adult and an infant.

Picture This
Scripture: Psalm 23

This Game Teaches: Important images and symbols of the Christian faith.

Supervision Tip: Monitor infants since they may try to rip the pictures and place pieces in their mouths.

Materials: Clear packing tape and colorful pictures relating to the Christian faith, such as a picture of Jesus, a picture of a church (or your church), a cross, a big red heart

Game: Tape pictures to the floor for babies to see as they crawl around. Choose pictures that are well-known symbols of the Christian faith. Use clear packing tape and cover each entire picture, if possible. Crawl on the floor with the baby as you play this game. Point to one picture and identify it. (For example, "Here is a picture of Jesus. We love Jesus at our church.") Continue to crawl around the room and identify more pictures. Once you've identified all the pictures, ask the baby, "Where's Jesus?" See if the baby knows. If not, crawl over to that picture and point to it. Then ask the baby again, "Where's Jesus?" This time the baby may know.

Some churches keep pictures like these taped to the floor so that babies can crawl over them and look at them, becoming more familiar with important symbols and images of the Christian faith.

End the game by saying, "We're at church. When we're at church, we worship Jesus." You can also quote a portion of Psalm 23, such as verse 6, if you wish. Then say, "I'm glad you come to our church."

1

Bonus Idea

If someone at your church has a digital camera, ask him or her to take photos of your church building, your worship area, the pastor, the adults who frequently staff the infant room, and other symbols of your church. Print out these images and tape them to the floor so that babies can begin to make connections between your church (and the people who are there) and the symbols of their faith.

Chase and Catch
Scripture:
1 Corinthians 9:24-27

2

This Game Teaches: Determination to do well.

Supervision Tip: Adjust your pace to challenge the baby without frustrating him or her.

Materials: None

Game: Get down on your hands and knees. Crawl toward a baby who is adept at crawling. When you get close to the baby, say, "I'm going to catch you!" Crawl up to the baby and give the baby a hug.

Encourage the baby to chase you. Ask, "Can you catch me?"

Crawl ahead a bit while watching the baby. If the baby doesn't move, ask the question again and take another step. Once the baby starts to crawl toward you, adjust your pace so that the baby has to crawl to catch you. Let the baby catch you. Then hug the baby.

Continue to play the game as long as the baby is excited to chase or be chased. (Typically it takes a bit for babies to figure out the game, but once they do, babies love to play this over and over.)

End the game by saying, "You chased me, and you caught me! I chased you, and I caught you! It's fun to play when we're determined to have fun and do well."

Mountaintop Praise
Scripture: Isaiah 42:10-12

This Game Teaches: A way to praise God

Supervision Tip: Watch the older babies (nine months or older) as they climb since they're more skilled at going up than at coming down.

Materials: A stairway somewhere in your church

Game: Find a stairway in your church that an older baby can climb up. (You might want to start with a shorter staircase and then gradually work your way to a longer flight of stairs.) At the bottom of the stairs, place the baby on his or her hands and knees. Encourage the baby to crawl up the stairs to the top while you watch him or her closely.

When the baby reaches the top, scoop the baby up in your arms and say, "Praise God! You reached the top!"

Carry the baby down the stairs and stop at the bottom. See if the baby wants to climb up the stairs again. (Most do, and many like to do this over and over.) Each time you reach the top, scoop up the baby and say, "Praise God! You reached the top!"

End the game by saying: "We shouted from the top and praised God. Wherever we are, we can praise God. I praise God for being able to spend time with you."

God Made All of You

Scripture: Matthew 10:29-31

This Game Teaches: God created each one of us and knows each one of us intimately.

Supervision Tip: Make eye contact with baby as you play this game.

Materials: None

Game: Take off baby's socks to expose his or her toes. Smile and point to each toe one by one while you sing this song to the tune of "Ten Little Indians":

(Verse 1)
One little, two little, three little toes-ies
Four little, five little, six little toes-ies
Seven little, eight little, nine little toes-ies
You have ten little toes.

Sing the song again, pointing to each finger, using these lyrics:

(Verse 2)
One little, two little, three little fingers
Four little, five little, six little fingers
Seven little, eight little, nine little fingers
Ten fingers on your hands.

End the game by saying: "God made all of you, your ten little fingers, your ten little toes, your eyes, your head, your nose. Let's clap for God for making you."

4

Rise on Wings Like Eagles
Scripture: Isaiah 40:29-31

This Game Teaches: Trust God and God will give you strength.

Supervision Tip: Keep a baby safe by having a firm hold on him or her. Never throw a baby up into the air.

Materials: None

Game: Using the classic airplane or football hold (where you hold a baby tummy down over your arm and support his or her chest with your hand so that baby seems to be flying), play this game. Guide the baby gently as you walk around the room, so that baby feels like he or she is flying. (Note: Only do this activity with babies who have developed their neck muscles so that they can hold up their head.)

Gently swing as you move the baby around the room. Say: "You're flying like an eagle. Flying higher and higher, and to and fro. Look at you fly and look at you go." End the game by saying:

"Those who trust in the LORD for help
    will find their strength renewed.
They will rise on wings like eagles;
    they will run and not get weary;
    they will walk and not grow weak." (Isaiah 40:31 GNT)

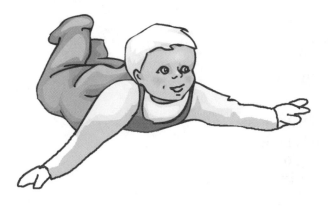

Up and Down
Scripture: Mark 2:1-12

This Game Teaches: Love of friends

Supervision Tip: Make sure both adults have a firm grip on the blanket.

Materials: One blanket

Game: Get a baby blanket and have two adults hold both ends of the blanket to create a hammock for the baby.

Place the baby blanket on the floor. Set one baby on his or her back in the middle of the blanket. Have one adult stand near the baby's head and the other near the baby's feet. Encourage the adult who is near the baby's feet to make eye contact and smile during the game.

Have both adults slowly lift up their ends of the blanket at the same time. Gently swing the baby back and forth like the baby is in a hammock. Monitor the baby's reaction so that you swing at the right pace for the baby.

As you swing, sing this to the tune of "The Farmer in the Dell":

(Verse 1)
The baby swings with us.
The baby swings with us.
Hi-ho the derry-o,
The baby swings with us.

(Verse 2)
We lift the baby high.
We lift the baby high.
Hi-ho the derry-o,
We lift the baby high.

(Verse 3)
We swing the baby more.
We swing the baby more.
Hi-ho the derry-o,
We swing the baby more.

6

(Verse 4)
We bring the baby down.
We bring the baby down.
Hi-ho the derry-o,
We bring the baby down.

End the game by saying: "A paralyzed man in the Bible had friends who lifted him up in a stretcher and lowered him down through a hole in the roof so that he could see Jesus. Friends can help us in all that we do, just like we played with you."

Bonus Tip

Babies like to hear their name in song. Instead of singing "the baby" during this song, substitute the child's name. If the child has a one-syllable name, sing "our friend Jeff." If the child has a two-syllable name, sing the child's name but have the second syllable take up two beats, such as "Tyrone swings with us." If the child has a three-syllable name, just substitute the name, such as "Maria swings with us."

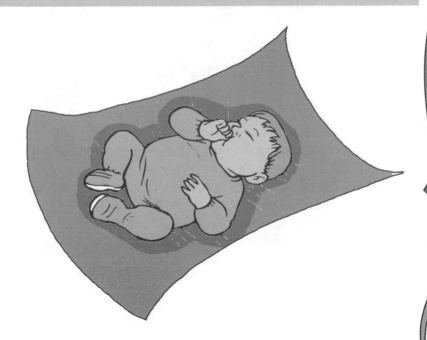

Learning More and More
Scripture: Ecclesiastes 7:11-12

This Game Teaches: Babies are wise and learning more each day.

Supervision Tip: Play this game with infants who are nine months and older.

Materials: None

Game: Ask an older baby (nine months or older) where specific items are in the room. For example, ask, "Where is the table?" With the baby in your lap or near you, ask about the placement of items in the room such as:

- Crib
- High chair
- Changing table
- Toy box
- Door
- Stroller
- A person (such as another nursery worker or another child in the room)

Pause each time you name something and watch what the baby does. Some babies will look in the direction of the object. A few may point or try to crawl in that direction. When the baby looks at the correct object, congratulate him or her and go over to the object together to touch it.

End the game by saying: "You're learning so much! God loves it when you learn more and more things."

Happy All the Time
Scripture: James 5:13

This Game Teaches: It's great to sing songs of praise and be happy.

Supervision Tip: Be upbeat and smile as you play with infants.

Materials: None

Game: You can do this game no matter what you're doing with the baby, such as feeding him or her, changing a diaper, or rocking him or her. Be upbeat. Just smile and be close to the baby while you're singing this song to the tune of "Are You Sleeping?"

"Are you eating? Are you eating?"

"Baby Ann? Baby Ann?" If the child has a two-syllable name, sing "Carlos, dear; Carlos dear." If the child has a three-syllable name, just sing the name, such as "Jer-em-y; Jer-em-y."

"I am glad you're with us; I am glad you're with us,"

"Baby Ann. Baby Ann."

Change the first verse to "Are you playing?" "Are you sleepy?" "Are you awake now?" "Let's get new clothes," "Are you hungry?" to fit the baby's activity. Then do the routine in a playful way as you sing. For example, make a dancing motion with a spoonful of food during eating or bounce a diaper up and down before putting it on the baby.

End the game by saying: "The Bible says, 'Is anyone happy? Let him sing songs of praise' " (James 5:13 NIV). Say: "I'm happy. I'm happy to be with you."

8

Crown Your Head
Scripture: Esther 2:16-18

This Game Teaches: When Esther found favor with the king, she was crowned queen.

Supervision Tip: Remove a hat immediately if babies get scared when a hat falls over their eyes and they can't see.

Materials: A variety of hats, a mirror

Game: Surround a baby with a variety of hats and a mirror. (You can also do this near a mirror.) Place one of the hats on the baby's head. Say, "Look at you! You have a hat on your head!" Give the baby a chance to respond. If the baby likes this, take off the hat and place another hat on the baby's head. (If the baby becomes upset, switch to another activity and try this again later.)

Each time you place a different hat on the baby's head, make positive remarks, such as "God thinks you look great, and I do too," "I crown you the queen (or king) of the room," "What kind of face can you make with that hat?"

Older babies (particularly ones who can sit up and have some mobility) may enjoy putting on the hats themselves. Try on hats together. Make faces. Laugh. Have fun.

End the game by saying: "In the Bible the king crowned Esther the queen and placed a crown on her head. I crown you Queen (or King) _____." (Say the baby's name as you place a hat on his or her head.)

Hidden Discoveries
Scripture: Matthew 7:7-8

This Game Teaches: Some great things in life may be hidden.

Supervision Tip: Ensure that the baby is alert to play this game and is fed, clean, and awake.

Materials: A favorite toy of the baby's and a blanket

Game: Place a blanket on the floor. Show the baby a favorite toy. While the baby is looking, place the toy halfway under the blanket so that part of the toy is hidden and part is in baby's view. (Even though this seems overly simplistic to adults, this actually is a developmental challenge for babies.) Ask, "Where's the toy?" (Or say the actual name of the toy.)

Some babies will point. Those who crawl may crawl over to get it. Some will even pull off the blanket to expose the entire toy. When the baby finds the toy, say, "You found it!"

Partially hide the toy under the other side of the blanket. Play the game again. Continue to repeat the game as long as baby wants to play.

End the game by saying, "The Bible says that whenever we look for something, we will find it. I asked you to look for the toy, and you found it."

Wonders of the World
Scripture: Job 37:14-16

11

This Game Teaches: The world is filled with wonderful things.
Supervision Tip: Supervise the baby to ensure that the bottles don't open and spill (contents could cause choking if placed in the baby's mouth).

    Materials: Two to three baby bottles, each partially filled with a different item, such as glitter, rice, buttons, beans, sequins, colorful paper clips, colored sand, or beads

    Game: Before you play the game, partially fill a baby bottle with one of the suggested items. Secure the top tightly so that the bottle will not open. Repeat this with one or two more bottles so that the baby has two to three bottles for the game.

Roll one of the bottles across the floor in front of a baby who is learning how to crawl or creep. Some babies will watch the bottle; others may try to chase after the bottle. To entice the baby to move, roll the bottle back toward the baby. Then show the baby how to roll the bottle back and forth.

Once the baby begins to play with the bottle, add another bottle. Then another, if you have a third. Some babies will roll the bottle and then crawl after it. Other babies will sit and roll the bottle back and forth. Affirm the baby for playing.

End the game by saying, "God makes many wonderful, colorful things."

Bonus Tip

Use different objects to brush the baby's cheek. Try a feather, a stuffed animal, a blanket, a small pillow, or something else that's soft. See how the baby reacts. As long as the baby smiles and enjoys the sensation, continue to play.

Tell the Good News
Scripture: Mark 1:14-15

This Game Teaches: To encourage the baby to vocalize and tell the good news.

Supervision Tip: Supervise the baby so that he or she doesn't chew on the paper towel tube or hit someone with it.

Materials: Two empty paper towel tubes (one for you and one for the baby)

Game: Sit near a baby. Pick up an empty paper towel tube and make noise through it, mimicking the language the baby uses (such as ma, ma, ma or da, da, da or ba, ba, ba). Give the other empty paper towel tube to the baby and encourage him or her to make sound in it.

Make different sounds into the tube and see if baby will follow:

- sing
- make low sounds
- make high sounds

Then say into the tube (or sing): "Good news! Good news! _____ (name of baby) is telling the good news!"

End the game by saying: "God likes it when we tell the good news. As you learn to talk more and more, you'll be able to tell the good news."

12

41

The Joy of Finding Baby Moses

Scripture: Exodus 2:1-10

This Game Teaches: Moses was loved and cared for after he was found.

Supervision Tip: Always support the neck and head of a young baby.

Materials: Baby blanket

Game: Because babies (particularly newborns) have weak neck muscles and need to develop those muscles to lift up and hold their heads, use this game to strengthen those muscles.

Lay the baby on his or her back on top of a blanket. Cradle one of your arms around the back of the baby to support his or her head and neck. Slowly pull the baby toward you in a gentle sit-up fashion. As you sing this song, slowly lift the baby up and lower the baby down, as if the baby were doing sit-ups with your help.

Sing to the tune of "Baa Baa Black Sheep":

Moses, Moses, hid down low
Come up closer, nice and slow.
I will care and love you too
That's what God says we should do.
Moses, Moses, hid down low
Come up closer, nice and slow.

End the game by saying: "People found baby Moses and took care of him, just like we take care of you."

13

A Big Goal
Scripture: Philippians 3:12-14

This Game Teaches: The enjoyment of achievement

Supervision Tip: Pace the game and monitor the infant's frustration levels.

Materials: A stuffed animal and a piece of furniture (or ledge for the baby to hold on to)

Game: Once a baby starts holding on to furniture and ledges for support to walk, play this game to encourage the baby to practice even more. Place a stuffed animal about one foot away from the baby on a piece of furniture (or ledge). Encourage the baby to walk to the stuffed animal. When he or she reaches it, hug the baby and say, "You did it!"

Play the game again, moving the stuffed animal farther away. Repeat the game while moving the stuffed animal farther away until the baby starts at one end of the furniture and the stuffed animal is at the other end. After the baby gets to the animal, hug the baby and say, "You did it!"

End the game by saying: "God likes it when we work hard to reach our goals. You walked to the stuffed animal every time! I'm so proud of you."

Bonus Tip

Adapt this game for younger babies who can at least crawl or creep by placing a loved toy out of their reach to see if they will move to get it. For even younger infants, hold the baby in your arms and place a stuffed animal onto their belly and then slowly move it away before you bring it back to their belly. (Some infants will reach out for the stuffed animal and smile.)

14

Push the Ark of the Covenant
Scripture: Joshua 3

This Game Teaches: Obedience

Supervision Tip: Keep the floor clear of clutter and spills so that baby doesn't slip.

Materials: A laundry basket and toys to place inside

Game: Fill up a laundry basket full of toys and stuffed animals. (Make sure it's heavy enough that it doesn't tip over but not too heavy for a baby to push.)

Encourage a baby who is walking or just beginning to walk to grab one side of the basket. Have an adult grab the other side. At first, gently pull the basket toward you and see what the baby does. Some may slightly lose their balance and then catch themselves. Others will quickly see that they can push this basket around the room.

As soon as the baby figures out that he or she can do this, encourage the baby to push the basket around. Applaud the efforts as the baby moves throughout the room.

End the game by saying: "God told the Israelites to cross the Jordan River and bring the ark of the covenant with them, and the people obeyed. You just acted out that story by pushing the basket!"

15

The Wonders of Sight
Scripture: Luke 10:23

This Game Teaches: Visual tracking skills

Supervision Tip: Keep small objects (such as pom-poms and cotton balls) out of reach of infants since they'll place these items into their mouths.

Materials: Bright-colored, large pom-poms (or colored cotton balls) and/or a handkerchief or scarf

Game: When babies are born, they don't have the visual skills of following objects with their eyes. These skills slowly develop over time. With a baby lying on his or her back, take a large pom-pom (or colored cotton ball) and hold it about twelve to fifteen inches away from the baby's face. Slowly move the pom-pom from the left side of the baby to the right side while the baby follows the pom-pom with his or her eyes.

Once the baby has mastered this, try moving the pom-pom close to the baby's face and then farther away. Gently swipe the baby's cheek with the pom-pom while you say upbeat remarks, such as "Look at your cute little cheeks," or "God made a perfect you with perfect cheeks." Then brush the pom-pom against other parts of the baby's body: the belly, toes, hands, or chin.

Repeat with a handkerchief or scarf (after you put away the pom-pom so that the baby cannot reach it and attempt to eat it). Hold the scarf about twelve to fifteen inches away from the baby's head. Swing it from side to side. Gently lower the scarf and brush it across the baby's face.

End the game by saying: "Jesus says in the Bible, 'How fortunate you are to see the things you see' " (Luke 10:23b GNT). Say: "I'm happy to see you, and I'm happy that your eyes are seeing more and more!"

16

Clap and Praise
Scripture:
2 Chronicles 5:11-14

This Game Teaches: Praise God through clapping.
Supervision Tip: Continue the game for as long as the baby enjoys it.

Materials: None

17

Game: Babies love to clap their hands (and have their hands clapped gently inside the hands of an adult if they haven't learned the skill yet). Sit with the baby on your lap and sing this song to the tune of "If You're Happy and You Know It":

(Verse 1)
If you're happy and you praise God, clap your hands (clap, clap)
If you're happy and you praise God, clap your hands (clap, clap)
If you're happy and you know it, then your claps will surely
   show it
If you're happy and you praise God, clap your hands (clap, clap)

Repeat the song again, using the following verses, which all emphasize different actions to do with the baby's hands:

(Verse 2)
If you're happy and you praise God, clap your legs (clap, clap)
If you're happy and you praise God, clap your legs (clap, clap)
If you're happy and you know it, then your claps will surely
   show it
If you're happy and you praise God, clap your legs (clap, clap)

(Verse 3)
If you're happy and you praise God, tap your face (clap, clap)
If you're happy and you praise God, tap your face (clap, clap)
If you're happy and you know it, then your taps will surely
   show it
If you're happy and you praise God, tap your face (clap, clap)

(Verse 4)
If you're happy and you praise God, clap your arms (clap, clap)
If you're happy and you praise God, clap your arms (clap, clap)
If you're happy and you know it, then your claps will surely
   show it
If you're happy and you praise God, clap your arms (clap, clap)

(Verse 5)
If you're happy and you praise God, clap your feet (clap, clap)
If you're happy and you praise God, clap your feet (clap, clap)
If you're happy and you know it, then your claps will surely
   show it
If you're happy and you praise God, clap your feet (clap, clap)

End the game by saying: "In the Bible, people praised God. We
praised God by clapping our hands, legs, face, arms, and feet."

Where Did They Go?
Scripture: Luke 15

This Game Teaches: There is joy in finding something that has disappeared.

Supervision Tip: Supervise babies at all times when you play games that have ribbons, yarn, or shoelaces to keep babies from choking.

Materials: Ribbons, yarn, or shoelaces to fasten infant toys (three to four of them) to a high chair table

18

Game: Infants love to drop toys and push them over the side of a high chair table. To give them a sense of mastery that they can then find these items again (without you having to pick them up), secure three to four infant toys (such as rattles and stuffed animals) each to a different ribbon (or yarn or shoelace) before fastening them to a high chair table.

Place the baby in the high chair (for a play time, not a feeding time). Place the three or four items on the high chair table for baby. At first the baby may play with these items, but eventually the baby will push these items off. When he or she does, say in a cheerful, playful voice, "Oh! Oh! Where did they go? Are they lost?"

Sometimes a baby will look over the side of the high chair. Say, "Look! We can find these things that are lost." Stand next to the baby and slowly pull one of the ribbons until the toy pops up over the edge. Do the same with the other ribbons. Eventually the baby will catch on that he or she can push toys over and pull them up again.

End the game by saying: "In the Bible, people were sad when they lost things. They lost sheep, a coin, even a boy! When they found what they had lost, they were so happy."

Funny Faces, Happy Sounds

Scripture:
Song of Songs 2:14*b*

This Game Teaches: Make different faces and vocalize.
Supervision Tip: Play as long as the baby enjoys this game.
Materials: A mirror
Game: Stand before a mirror with the baby. (Or get a mirror that the two of you can look into together.) Babies love to mimic the faces that people make, and many babies also will make faces for you to mimic. Take turns making faces into the mirror.
* Wrinkle your nose
* Smile and show your teeth
* Stick out your tongue
* Throw kisses (where you place a hand on your lips, make a kissing sound, and throw out your hand toward the mirror)
* Contort your lips into different shapes
Then make sounds into the mirror along with your funny face:
* Laugh (and open your mouth wide)
* Squeal (and close your eyes)
* Sing (and move your tongue in and out of your mouth)
End the game by saying: "In the Bible it says, 'Let me see your lovely face / and hear your enchanting voice'" (Song of Songs 2:14*b* GNT). "I saw the many, many lovely faces you made. I heard all the beautiful sounds you could make. God loves all your beautiful faces and loves to hear you talk and sing."

19

The Whole Body
Scripture: Luke 11:33-36

This Game Teaches: Enjoy the body God has given us.

Supervision Tip: Monitor the infant as you play this game to see how long he or she wants to play.

Materials: An inflatable beach ball

Game: Place the baby on his or her back on the floor. Kneel by the baby, your knees near the baby's feet so that you can make eye contact with the baby.

Starting at the baby's feet, slowly roll an inflatable beach ball up the baby to his or her neck. If the baby tries to grab the ball or kick it, let him or her do so. Once you get to the baby's neck, roll the ball back down the baby's body to his or her feet. Continue to move the ball up and down the baby's body while monitoring the baby's reactions.

As you play this game, sing this to the tune of "Row, Row, Row Your Boat":

(Verse 1)
Up, up, up, we roll
Right up to your face
Nice and slow, nice and slow
We move the ball with grace.

(Verse 2)
Down, down, down, we roll
Down the ball now goes
Feel the ball, feel the ball
Right back to your toes.

(Verse 3)
Up, up, up, we roll
When will we be done?
Not until, not until
We smile and have some fun.

20

End the game by saying, "You felt the ball go up and down the beautiful body that God made. I love your toes (touch the baby's toes), your legs (touch the baby's legs), your tummy (touch the baby's tummy), your arms (touch the baby's arms), and your face (gently touch the baby's face). I love everything about you that God made."

Fun Games for Young Toddlers
(From 1 to 2 Years)

Young toddlers find the world a fascinating place and explore it from top to bottom, which is why adults say that this age group is into everything. Most toddlers usually entertain themselves with what they stumble upon, but they periodically need an adult to direct their attention to a game or another activity to distract them from mischief or harm.

Playing with a young toddler works best if you delight in what they discover, not in what they attempt to master. When toddlers use a plastic hammer to insert play nails into a play shoe, they'll become more interested in the banging sounds and the feel of the hammer as they pound rather than in what they hit or miss.

When you talk about God's love, start first with what toddlers experience. For example say, "Mom loves you. I love you. God loves you," while you hug the toddler. (Do this when a toddler is open to affection, not when she or he is absorbed in another activity.)

As you play with a young toddler, let the toddler take the lead. Start the game and see what develops. Sometimes you'll get to the end of the game, other times you won't because something else will catch a young toddler's attention. That's okay. The three major goals for playing with a young toddler include interacting with young toddlers in playful, loving ways; introducing simple Bible stories and concepts to them; and having fun. Getting from the beginning of a game to the end is something adults like to do, not young toddlers. As long as young toddlers enjoy being with you and find the game or activity interesting, you're moving in the right direction in developing a young toddler's spiritual life.

The Sound of the Good News
Scripture: Matthew 28:16-20

This Game Teaches: Communication is key.

Supervision Tip: Make eye contact with the toddler as you play this game.

Materials: None

Game: Sit on the floor with a young toddler, facing the child. When the child says something, like "da-da-da," repeat back to the child what he or she said, such as "da-da-da." Toddlers often will say "da-da-da" again since they enjoy communicating with someone.

Play the game again, but this time change your response slightly, such as "doh-doh-doh" or "duh-duh-duh," and see if the child will mimic the sound that you made. (Many children will try this.)

Whatever happens, make facial expressions and play along as if the two of you are having a delightful conversation. (Toddlers enjoy this greatly.)

End the game by saying: "I love talking to you. In the Bible, it says to tell the good news. You told me lots of great news by the way you talk."

Cuddly Creatures
Scripture: Genesis 30:25-43

This Game Teaches: We can care for animals (even stuffed animals).

Supervision Tip: Periodically inspect stuffed animals for tears and loose pieces.

Materials: Stuffed animals

Game: Sit on the floor and face a young toddler. Place a few stuffed animals in between the two of you. Pick up one of the stuffed animals, such as a teddy bear. Hug it tight. Cuddle it, and say, "I love you, teddy." Gently pat the animal and say, "I love your brown fur." Look closely into the animal's eyes and say, "I love your cute little eyes."

Then look at the child. Hug the child. Say, "I love you (name of child)." Point out different aspects of the child that you love, such as his or her hair, fingers, nose, and so forth.

Give one of the stuffed animals to the child. Say: "Show me how much you love this animal. Can you cuddle it and hug it?" Encourage the child to give the stuffed animal kisses.

Ask how much the child loves the other stuffed animals. Some children will show love and affection to each of the other stuffed animals one by one. Others may try to scoop all of them up and hug them at the same time. Enjoy how the child shows affection.

As you play, sing this to the refrain, "Yes, Jesus loves me," from the song "Jesus Loves Me":

Who can we cuddle?
Who can we cuddle?
Who can we cuddle?
To love is wonderful.

End the game by saying, "In the Bible, Jacob takes good care of the animals. It's great to care for and love real animals and stuffed animals."

22

Body Wise
Scripture:
1 Corinthians 12:12-31

This Game Teaches: Every part of the body is important—and essential.

Supervision Tip: Monitor young toddlers since most struggle with coordination and can accidentally hurt themselves when touching their eyes or other body parts.

Materials: None

Game: Ask a young toddler to stand while you sit in front of him or her. (That way you can easily make eye contact with the child.) Ask the child the following:

• Where are your hands? Can you touch your hands?
• Where are your feet? Can you touch your feet?
• Where is your head? Can you touch your head?
• Where is your tummy? Can you touch your tummy?

Pay attention to how well the child knows his or her body parts. (This learning comes slowly and gradually.) If the child seems to know more, ask about more specific body parts, such as ears, fingers, knees, mouth, nose, toes, and eyes. (Don't be concerned, however, if the child doesn't know where some of these body parts are. If you wish, you can show the child where one or two more body parts are.)

End the game by saying, "God made our bodies, and each part is important. I love your hands (touch the child's hands), your feet (touch the child's feet), your head (touch the child's head), and your tummy (touch the child's tummy). I love everything about you." (Hug the child.)

Match This, Match That
Scripture: Ezra 1

This Game Teaches: God's people took inventory of items King Nebuchadnezzar stole.

Supervision Tip: Monitor toddlers so they don't poke themselves or others with the objects.

Materials: One piece of white posterboard, a black marker, and items for toddlers to play with, such as a bowl, a cup, a fork, a spoon, a knife, a saucer (or plate).

Game: Before the game, trace each item (the bowl, the cup, the fork, the spoon, the knife, the saucer) onto the posterboard with a marker. (You're creating outlines of all these items for toddlers to match with the actual item.)

When you're ready to play, ask a toddler to sit in front of the posterboard. Place all the items in a pile near the posterboard. Say: "Can you find this item?" Point to one of the outlines that's easy to identify, such as a fork. Encourage the toddler to look through the pile of items until he or she locates the piece. Then have the toddler place the item onto the outline on the posterboard.

Continue to encourage the toddler to find matching items. If the toddler becomes stuck, encourage him or her to put the item down and choose another one to try. Play until the entire posterboard is covered with the items.

End the game by saying: "In the Bible, the people of God found all the bowls and cups that the bad king had stolen. Then they put them back into their church. You found everything and returned them to their proper place."

24

A Lot to Harvest
Scripture: Luke 10:2

This Game Teaches: We can help gather in the harvest when it is ready.

Supervision Tip: Monitor the items that toddlers pick up and collect; adult supervisors may find their keys or other valuables missing (and hidden in the container for this game).

Materials: An empty cardboard six-pack soda-pop container, cotton balls spread throughout the room

Game: Before you play this game, spread cotton balls throughout your room or play area. Give a toddler an empty cardboard six-pack, soda-pop container. Say: "Look what I've found!" Pick up one cotton ball. Place it into one of the spots in the six-pack container. Say: "How many of these cotton balls can you find and collect?"

Encourage the toddler to walk around and collect the cotton balls, placing them into one of the six spaces in his or her container. As the child plays this game, sing this to the tune of "Mary Had a Little Lamb":

(Verse 1)
Look to see what you can find
You can find, you can find
Look to see what you can find
And put them in your box.

(Verse 2)
I can see another one
'nother one, 'nother one
I can see another one
You're getting very close (or: You're getting far away).

(Verse 3)
Look you found them all today
All today, all today

25

Look you found them all today
You picked up every one.

End the game by saying: "Many people in the Bible gathered the harvest when it was ready. Jesus often talked metaphorically about the harvest. I'm proud that you found so many cotton balls and picked them all up."

Bonus Tip

Cover the empty cardboard six-pack, soda-pop container with a decorative contact paper. Consider letting toddlers play with the container during their free time since children at this age love gathering things and placing them into containers.

Have a Ball
Scripture:
Ecclesiastes 11:9-10

26

This Game Teaches: Have fun and enjoy being together.

Supervision Tip: Be clear that throwing the ball is not okay (and can hit someone or something).

Materials: A lightweight rubber ball

Game: Sit on the floor facing a young toddler with your legs stretched out in front of you. Help the toddler stretch out his or her legs. Sit close together so that your legs form a playing area between the two of you.

Take a lightweight rubber ball. Roll it to the toddler. Say, "I roll the ball to (child's name)." Encourage the child to stop the ball and roll it back to you. When he or she rolls it toward you, say, "(Child's name) rolls the ball to (your name)."

Continue rolling the ball back and forth to each other, saying the child's name and your name as you roll.

End the game by saying, "Being a toddler is a great thing. I had a ball rolling the ball back and forth with you."

Follow, Follow
Scripture: John 1:35-51

This Game Teaches: Listen and follow the leader.

Supervision Tip: Keep an eye on toddlers as they walk (since they love to pick up things and put things in their mouths or poke their fingers into holes and interesting places).

Materials: A roll of crepe paper (or streamers), masking tape

Game: Take one to three young toddlers on a walk. (Take more if you have extra adult supervision.) Bring the crepe paper and masking tape with you.

As you walk, periodically stop. Tear off a piece of crepe paper. Place a piece of masking tape on the end and ask one of the toddlers to hang it somewhere nearby (such as on the wall). Say, "We're making a trail of color. When we return from our walk, we'll look for the colors to show us our way back to the room."

Continue on your walk. Stop once in a while to have a toddler hang up the next piece of crepe paper. (While you do this, keep track of your trail so that you can lead the way back.)

After you have hung up five to ten pieces of crepe paper, turn the group around. Say, "We're going back to our room. Can we find the way? Who sees one of our colored markings?" Count the crepe paper pieces as you find them and remove them from the wall.

End the game by saying, "In the Bible, Jesus asked people to follow him. You did a great job of following me and the pieces of colored crepe paper."

27

Bonus Idea

On a warm day, take the toddlers outside to play this game. Mark your path by placing crepe paper pieces on trees, sides of buildings or cars (but stick tape on mirrors and other surfaces that won't remove any paint), playground equipment, or fences. As you play, talk about God's creation.

Open My Eyes
Scripture: Psalm 119:18

This Game Teaches: Toddlers can become more aware of what they see around them.

Supervision Tip: Even though toddlers have short attention spans, some toddlers have longer attention spans than others do. Work with their attention span instead of against it.

Materials: None

Game: If your church sanctuary is empty (or your church has a small chapel), take young toddlers to see what's there. (Most young toddlers have seen only the pews or chairs of a sanctuary.) Show toddlers other parts of the sanctuary that they haven't seen before.

As you show toddlers the sanctuary, ask, "What do you see?" Encourage toddlers to point and name what they see. Name objects and places they don't recognize. Follow toddlers to find out what interests them. Encourage toddlers to talk as you play the game.

End the game by saying, "When we open our eyes and notice what's around us, we see so much more. You saw all kinds of new things today. I wonder what we will see next."

Bonus Idea

Play this game in front of a window. Pull up a chair for yourself and a young toddler. Face the window and ask the child what he or she sees. If you see movement, ask the toddler about that, such as "Where do you think the car is going?" "Where do you think the plane is going?" "Where do you think the person is going?" The more young children notice what's going on around them and verbalize what they see and think, the more they will develop language and critical thinking skills.

28

Bigger Bubbles
Scripture: 1 Timothy 4:4

This Game Teaches: God created many wonderful things.

Supervision Tip: Monitor toddlers so they don't swallow soapy water.

Materials: A bowl, dishwashing liquid, water, straws, towels

Game: Fill a bowl about one quarter of the way with water. Give a toddler a straw and have him or her practice blowing through the straw (not sucking in) and then blowing air through the straw into the bowl of water. Once the toddler gets the hang of blowing into the water, add dishwashing liquid to the water. Encourage the child to blow again. (Longer-lasting bubbles will form, and many more will develop as the child continues to blow.)

Ask: "How many bubbles can you blow?" See what the toddler can do. Then ask: "Can you make bigger bubbles by blowing really hard?" (Water and bubbles may splash over the bowl.)

Let the child continue to play under close supervision. End the game by saying: "God made many great things: water, fun times, and bubbles. I love all the bubbles you made."

29

Who's in the Tent?
Scripture: Exodus 33:7-11

This Game Teaches: The Israelites lived in tents, and Moses visited God in the tent of the Lord.

Supervision Tip: Make sure that toddlers do not become scared or entangled in blankets.

Materials: A few chairs and blankets (or sheets); optional: a large box

Game: Create a couple of tents by placing a few chairs together and draping a blanket or sheet over the top. (Or if you have a large box, set it up on its side and drape a blanket over the entrance.)

Encourage a toddler (or two) to crawl into the tents. Once a toddler is hidden. Ask: "Where's (name of child)?" Continue to say things like, "I don't know where she is. She was just here a minute ago. Has anyone seen (name of child)?"

Often toddlers will giggle during this game as you look around. Then lift up the blankets one by one to see who is inside. Once you find the toddler, say, "Here you are! I found you!"

Play for as long as toddlers want to play. End the game by saying: "In the Bible, the Israelites lived in tents, and Moses visited God in a special tent. Today we pretended to be the Israelites by playing in our tents."

30

Spotless
Scripture: 2 Corinthians 7:1

This Game Teaches: We can purify ourselves for God.

Supervision Tip: Make sure children don't rub their eyes since shaving cream will irritate their eyes.

Materials: Shaving cream, towel, and either an empty tabletop or cookie sheet

Game: Locate a place for toddlers to play this game, such as an empty tabletop or a cookie sheet. (Some people prefer cookie sheets to try to contain the mess.)

Spray a little shaving cream on the top of the empty tabletop or cookie sheet. Ask the toddler to use his or her hands to spread the shaving cream around. (A few toddlers may resist since some toddlers don't like to get their hands dirty. That's okay. Most toddlers will jump right in.)

Ask: "Can you clean the whole table (or cookie sheet)?" Have toddlers cover the entire surface with shaving cream. Afterward, encourage them to draw pictures with their hands and fingers.

End the game by saying: "God wants us to purify and clean ourselves on the inside. Today we purified and cleaned the outside of the table (or cookie sheet). As you grow, you'll see how much our Bible talks about being whiter than snow, which is about keeping clean on the inside."

31

Tumbling Walls
Scripture: Joshua 6

This Game Teaches: God was with the Israelites when the walls of Jericho fell.

Supervision Tip: Keep toddlers safe from falling sponges.

Materials: About thirty dry dishwashing sponges

Game: Place about thirty dry sponges around a toddler. Show the toddler how to stack the sponges on top of each other, like a tower or stacking toy. If the toddler wants you to help, stack sponges with the toddler.

   As the toddler stacks sponges, say: "In the Bible, the people of Jericho didn't want the Israelites to come in so they kept their gates shut and the walls of the city tall. Right now we're building Jericho so that no one can get in."

When the sponge tower begins to wobble, say: "God told the Israelites that God would help them get into Jericho."

Be dramatic in your response as the sponges topple over. Say, "Boom! Bam! The walls of Jericho came tumbling down."

Many toddlers will laugh when the sponges fall and will want to stack the sponges again. Sing this song to the tune of "The Itsy, Bitsy Spider" as toddlers build again:

The bad guys built their walls tall to keep God's people out.
Down came the walls and splattered all about.
In came God's people to look around the town.
And they figured out that their God would never let them down.

End the game by saying: "God was with the Israelites when the walls of Jericho fell. God is with us as we play."

32

Seek and Peek
Scripture: Luke 11:9-10

This Game Teaches: God encourages us to seek and find.

Supervision Tip: Secure the mirror and fabric so that they don't fall on a toddler.

Materials: A mirror and a fabric cloth that will completely cover the mirror

Game: Before the game, find a secure place for a mirror near the floor. Rig up a fabric cloth to completely cover the mirror. (You may want to use a dowel to hold the top of the fabric cloth or try taping the top of the fabric cloth over the top edge of the mirror on the back with duct tape.)

33

Once the mirror and fabric cloth are secure, encourage a toddler to stand in front of the mirror. Ask: "Who's under there? Look and see." Encourage the toddler to lift up the cloth fabric. When he or she does, say, "Look! (Name of child) is there!"

Encourage the child to put the cloth down so that it covers the entire mirror. Ask the child again about who's under there. Most toddlers will enjoy peeking over and over. You can even play a game of peek-a-boo if you wish and use it with infants, too.

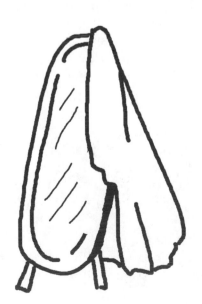

End the game by saying, "God encourages us to seek and find. Who did you find when you peeked under the cloth? You discovered a reflection of you!"

Wild Weather
Scripture: Job 37:1-6

This Game Teaches: God creates all kinds of weather.

Supervision Tip: Monitor toddlers so they don't throw balls around the room.

Materials: A large cardboard gift-wrap tube (or a mailing tube), table tennis balls, a bucket, a ball of yarn, scissors

34

Game: Cut pieces of yarn to tie a large cardboard gift-wrap tube to a banister or something that has a slant to it. (You want a toddler to be able to reach the highest end of the tube while standing.) Place a bucket on the floor near the end of the tube that is closest to the ground.

Ask a toddler to play. Give the toddler a table tennis ball and have the toddler drop the ball from the high end of the tube to see what happens. (The ball should roll down the tube, fall out the other end, and fall into the bucket. Make adjustments if needed.)

Say: "Let's pretend the ball is a raindrop. Can you make it rain into the bucket?" One by one, give the toddler table tennis balls to drop through the tube. Once the toddler grasps the concept, add more actions to the game:

• Jump up and down and yell "boom" for thunder.

• Have another adult hold his or her hand over the tube closest to the floor while the toddler fills up the tube with balls. Then have the toddler come to the bucket and watch as the adult lets go and a stream of balls fall in.

• Encourage the toddler to go to the light switch and make lightning by pushing the light switch up and down. (If the light switches are high, an adult may need to hold the child.)

Sing this to the tune of "London Bridge Is Falling Down":

(Verse 1)
Water drops are falling down, falling down, falling down
Water drops are falling down; it is raining.

(Verse 2)
Add some thunder to the storm, to the storm, to the storm
Add some thunder to the storm; Boom! Crash! Crackle!

(Verse 3)
See the lightning light the sky, light the sky, light the sky
See the lightning light the sky; then hear thunder.

End the game by saying: "God makes all kinds of weather: rain, sunshine, snow, storms, clouds. Let's thank God for the weather." Teach the toddler how to fold his or her hands together to pray. Say: "Thank you God for weather. Amen."

All Is Well
Scripture: Matthew 4:23-25

This Game Teaches: Jesus healed the sick.

Supervision Tip: Open the bandage packages before you play so that toddlers don't become frustrated when trying to open them.

Materials: A half of a box of inexpensive, small bandages for each child

35

Game: Say: "In the Bible, Jesus healed sick people. When you get an owie, what do you do?" (Listen to the toddler's ideas. Hopefully the toddler will mention bandages.)

Say: "Here are a lot of bandages. Let's pretend that we have a whole bunch of owies and that Jesus is helping us feel better." Encourage the toddler to place bandages on his or her arms, clothes, and skin. This is typically more fun if you have a lot of bandages.

End the game by saying: "Jesus healed the sick and helped them to feel better. Our bandages can remind us about what a good doctor Jesus was!"

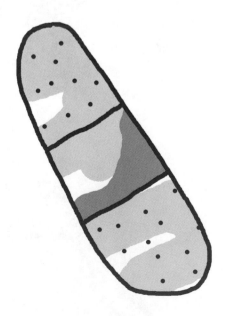

Make a Joyful Noise
Scripture: Psalm 150

This Game Teaches: We can praise God.

Supervision Tip: Ensure that containers are well secured so items don't fall out and pose a choking hazard.

Materials: Containers that have covers and can roll (such as potato chip cans or coffee cans), noisemakers to place inside the containers (such as jingle bells, small stones, or paper clips), duct tape

Game: Create music containers by placing one type of item (such as jingle bells) into a container with a cover. Secure lid with duct tape. If possible, make three or four different ones.

36

Give a toddler one of the containers. Say: "Let's make music for God!" Encourage the child to try different ways to make music, such as shaking the container, rolling the container across the floor, jumping up and down with the containers, and so on. Some toddlers will even enjoy singing while making this joyful noise (even if the singing isn't to any tune). Continue for as long as toddlers enjoy making music.

End the game by saying: "The Bible says it's great to praise God by making music. You made beautiful music for God."

Bonus Tip

Pet stores that sell aquariums often have inexpensive items (such as the colorful gravel for the bottom of fish tanks, small shells, or small plastic pebbles) that you can use in containers.

Symbols of Faith
Scripture: Hebrews 11

This Game Teaches: Symbols remind us of our faith.

Supervision Tip: Encourage toddlers not to rip or tear the pictures.

Materials: Photos (or digital photos printed on paper) of Christian symbols that you also have in your room or play area (symbols could include: a cross, a Bible, a star, a toy ark, an illustration of Jesus on your wall or door), large cardboard cards

Game: Before you play this game, add Christian symbols to your room or play area and take photos of them. Mount a photo of one item on each piece of cardboard so that you have a number of cards.

Hand one card to a child and say: "This is a picture of a cross. Can you find the real cross in our room?" Have the child look around the room, and then hold up the picture next to the real item.

Repeat the game with different cards until the child has found every object.

End the game by saying: "These are all symbols of our faith. The Bible says it's important that we grow in our faith."

Bonus Tip

If you have caregivers who regularly spend time with toddlers, take photographs of the caregivers and mount each one on a cardboard card. When you play the game, ask: "Where's (name of caregiver)?" and have the child find the caregiver who is in the picture.

37

What's in Your Purse?

Scripture: 1 Samuel 17:40

This Game Teaches: David (like many shepherds) used a purse or bag.

Supervision Tip: Monitor toddlers so they don't place items from the purse into their mouths.

Materials: A purse for toddlers to play with, five stones, and other items for a purse (such as play keys, wallet, small mirror, comb)

Game: Before you play this game, gather all the materials into the purse so that toddlers have a purse they can play with. Toddlers love opening a purse, dumping the contents, and putting the contents back in the purse (along with other things that may surprise you).

Play the game by giving the toddler a purse filled with items, including the five stones. Say: "What's inside the purse? What can you find?" Encourage the toddler to open the purse and see what's inside. As the toddler sees the items, identify them by naming what they are.

Then say: "What are these? Five stones? Why are there five stones in your purse? Does your mom carry stones in her purse?"

End the game by saying: "Lots of people carry a purse. Even people in the Bible carried a bag or a purse. David also carried five stones in his bag. David used the rocks to keep himself safe."

38

Ready for a Trip?
Scripture: Acts 14:21-28

This Game Teaches: Paul and Barnabas traveled to spread the good news.

Supervision Tip: Ensure that toddlers don't slam their fingers inside the suitcase.

Materials: A suitcase, play clothes

Game: Open up a suitcase. Say: "We're going on a trip like Paul and Barnabas. What should we pack for our trip?"

Encourage the toddler to walk around the room and find items to pack. Most toddlers will put in some play clothes, toys, and other objects. To add to the challenge of this game, ask the toddler to find a specific item in the room, such as a blue ball, a red telephone, or a teddy bear.

Once the suitcase is full, close it up and walk with the toddler across the room. Stop and open the suitcase. Say: "Here we are! Let's unpack our suitcase." Help the toddler put things away.

End the game by saying: "Paul and Barnabas took many trips to tell other people about Jesus. I like how you packed and unpacked our suitcase full of great things."

39

Amazing Rocks
Scripture:
Deuteronomy 8:11-20

This Game Teaches: God provides for our needs.

Supervision Tip: Keep toddlers safe by always monitoring them when they're around water.

Materials: A variety of rocks, dishwashing sponges, a bucket of water, towels

40

Game: Partially fill a bucket with water. Place a variety of rocks and the bucket of water in front of the toddler. Give the toddler a sponge. Say: "Can you wash one of the rocks? Dip your sponge into the bucket of water and wash your rock."

Encourage the toddler to wash only one rock. When he or she finishes, ask: "How does your wet rock look different from the dry rock?" (You may even want to pick up the two different rocks so the toddler can look closer.) Ask: "What happens if you dip your hand into the water and sprinkle water on a dry rock?" (Help the toddler do this.)

Then let the toddler wash all the rocks. When the toddler is finished, clean up the water with a towel.

End the game by saying: "The Bible talks a lot about rocks. In one story, God makes water flow out of a rock when the people didn't have any water. God always provides for us."

Section 3

Fun Games for
OLDER TODDLERS
(FROM 2 TO 3 YEARS)

Playing with an older toddler often can be more difficult for an adult than playing with a younger toddler. Due to the way children develop, the attention span for children at this age often seems shorter than for younger toddlers. Most of this is due to the more rapid, quiet growth going on inside the toddler's mind rather than in the body.

Older toddlers enthusiastically start most games that you initiate, but very few will finish them. They get distracted easily, and they wander off to other activities with ease. Instead of focusing on your hopes for an outcome of a game, join them in their distractions. Find out what interests them, whether it's the way a toy jumps out of a Jack-in-the-box or the path of a crawling ladybug.

As older toddlers develop and grow into young preschoolers, they become more versatile at play. Some mix music and rhythms with their play; others integrate more imagination into games. Their attention span slowly expands but will still remain quite short for another few years.

Remember that older toddlers still prefer to play with an adult. They will play alongside another toddler, but most of their play will be separate and solitary. As children grow, they will gradually interact more with their peers. Until then, capitalize on their interest in playing with an adult and enjoy your playtime together.

A Circle of Colors
Scripture:
1 Chronicles 29:1-9

41

This Game Teaches: King David gives colorful stones and gems for God's temple.

Supervision Tip: Ensure that the construction paper is secured to the floor so slipping and tripping doesn't occur.

Materials: 8 1/2 x 11 inch construction paper in red, yellow, and blue (four pieces of each color), masking tape

Game: Alternate the construction-paper colors so that they are in order of red, yellow, blue, red, yellow, blue, and so forth. Create a circle with the colors, and tape the colored pieces to the floor with masking tape.

Have a toddler stand on one of the pieces of paper. Ask the toddler which color he or she is standing on. If he or she doesn't know, tell the toddler what the name of the color is.

Say: "When I stop singing the song, stop on a piece of paper."

Begin to sing this to the tune of "Jack and Jill":

Here we walk around the circle
Looking as we caper
Is it red? Or is it blue?
What color is the paper?

Stop singing. Encourage the toddler to stop, if he or she has not done so. Ask: "What color are you standing on?" Once either the toddler or you have identified the color, repeat the game again as you sing and the toddler walks around the circle.

End the game by saying: "We all like lots of color. In the Bible, King David gave colorful stones and gems for God's temple. In this game, we played and learned more about red, yellow, and blue."

Bonus Idea

If your church has stained-glass windows or another colorful symbol, take toddlers to this part of the church to look at the symbol. Talk about how churches like to have colorful pictures to remind us of the colorful creation God has made and the sacred mystery of it all.

Jumping for Joy
Scripture: Acts 3:1-10

This Game Teaches: Peter heals a lame man.

Supervision Tip: Remove any items on the floor that may cause a toddler to trip.

Materials: Colored duct tape

Game: Mark an X on the floor with colored duct tape. (The color of the duct tape doesn't matter. Use a color that makes the X vivid and easy to see.)

42

Ask a toddler to stand about six inches away from the X marked on the floor. Say: "In the Bible, Peter healed a man who could not walk. When the man was healed, he got up, walked and jumped for joy. I want you to pretend you're that man and jump for joy by jumping onto the X on the floor."

Although this may seem simplistic, jumping is a skill that takes toddlers a long time to master. To jump well, toddlers need to learn to get a sense of balance, gain an awareness of where their body is spatially in relation to everything else, use gross-motor skills, and coordinate the movement between their eyes and feet.

Adjust the distance of where the child is standing depending on how far or close the child got when jumping onto the X. (If the child is afraid to jump, hold his or her hand.) Each time the toddler jumps, say, "Jump for joy! Jump for joy!"

As the toddler becomes more confident and skilled, he or she will often aim for the X over and over again.

End the game by saying, "We can praise and jump, just like the man who was healed in the Bible."

Then There Were People
Scripture: Genesis 1

This Game Teaches: God creates people.

Supervision Tip: Keep toddlers warm as you play outside in the snow.

Materials: A winter day with snow on the ground (preferably while it's snowing or recently after it has snowed), a big box of raisins, optional: a camera with film, and optional: pretzel sticks

43

Game: Bundle up toddlers in winter gear and bring them outside in the snow. Say: "Today we're going to create snow babies, just like God created people when God made the earth."

Show toddlers how to make snow babies. (Make three snowballs and place them on top of each other to make a snow baby.) Use small sticks (or pretzel sticks) for arms and raisins for facial features (the eyes, nose, and mouth). Encourage toddlers to make lots of babies, including big babies and small babies.

If you have a camera, take photographs of toddlers with their snow babies. (Snow babies will melt quickly so they won't stay around long.)

End the game by saying: "In the beginning, God made the heavens and the earth. God then made people. Wasn't it fun to make snow babies today?"

Love All Around

Scripture: 1 Corinthians 13

This Game Teaches: Love one another.

Supervision Tip: Watch toddlers' moods since upset toddlers may tear up paper hearts.

Materials: Red construction paper, scissors, a basket, glue, a white piece of posterboard, masking tape

Game: Before you play the game, cut hearts out of red construction paper. If possible cut out about twenty red hearts in different sizes. Place all except one of the hearts around the room. Hide them so that they're easy to find.

Give a toddler a basket and the one red heart you kept behind. Say: "I love you. When we talk about love, we often have a big red heart like this one." Point around the room, and say, "There are lots of hearts around the room. Can you find them and put them in your basket?"

Walk with the toddler as he or she places hearts into the basket. As you walk together, sing a song about love, such as the theme song "I Love You" from the PBS show *Barney & Friends,* or the well-known Christian children's song "Jesus Loves the Little Children."

After the toddler fills the basket, count the hearts together. Hang up a piece of posterboard with masking tape. Hold the glue bottle and ask the toddler to give you one heart. Place a dab of glue on the back of the heart. Give it to the toddler to place anywhere on the posterboard. Fill up the poster-board with all the hearts. If you wish, give the posterboard to the toddler's parents or hang it up in your room.

End the game by saying: "Love is what we're all about. God loves you. I love you."

44

A Rainbow of Color
Scripture: Genesis 9

This Game Teaches: God created a rainbow of color and a rainbow of promise.

Supervision Tip: Make sure toddlers keep eyedroppers out of their mouths.

Materials: Eyedroppers; white ice cube tray; water; food coloring in red, yellow, and blue (the kind where it's easy to use one drop of color at a time)

Game: Partially fill a white ice cube tray with water. Place two drops of red food coloring in one compartment. Place two drops of yellow food coloring in one of the middle compartments, and place two drops of blue food coloring at the opposite end of the tray from the red.

Give the toddler an eyedropper. Demonstrate how to use the eyedropper with clear water from one of the other compartments. Let the child practice until he or she knows how to use an eyedropper.

Encourage the child to transfer color from one compartment to another. Ask the child what happens if he or she moves some of the red into one place and then adds some yellow to the same place. (The child will create orange.) Give the child time to experiment and play. (Don't be surprised, however, if all the containers turn a brownish-black by the end of the game.)

Finish the game by saying: "God created all the colors of the rainbow. Let's clap for God for making all these great colors!" (Clap together.)

Bonus Tip

If you can keep containers with separate colors (ideally with blue, red, yellow, orange, green, and purple) consider giving children paper towels and letting them transfer the colored water onto the paper towels using the eyedropper. Children will enjoy watching how the color spreads (from the paper towel absorbing the color).

45

Lost and Found
Scripture: Matthew 18:12-14

This Game Teaches: We each count with Jesus.

Supervision Tip: Remove any wind-up toys from children after the game if you fear that they could break the wind-up mechanism.

Materials: A stuffed animal (a lamb if possible) that has a wind-up music box inside

46

Game: Show a child a stuffed animal that has a wind-up music box. Play the music for him or her. Say: "Do you see the (name of animal)? Do you hear the music?"

Wind up the music box more and hurry across the room. Let the child watch as you hide the stuffed animal while the music continues to play. Then return to the child and get down on your knees on the floor next to him or her.

Ask: "Where's the (name of animal)? Where's the music?" As the child walks across the room, crawl with the child (or walk on your knees so that you're closer to the child's level). Make the traveling time fun and be excited when the child finds the musical toy.

Some children may even try to hide the animal to mimic your action. Others may try to start up the music once it stops. If so, play along and affirm the child for what he or she tries to do.

After the game, say: "Jesus loves us so much that we can never get lost for long. When a sheep got lost, Jesus went looking for it until he brought it back safely. We're always safe with Jesus."

Dazzling Dress-Up
Scripture: Ezekiel 16:9-14

This Game Teaches: We can enjoy clothes and jewelry as long as having them doesn't sidetrack us.

Supervision Tip: Examine dress-up clothes and jewelry and make any necessary repairs.

Materials: Dress-up clothes, jewelry, shoes, crown (if possible)

Game: Before you play the game, create a dress-up area or fill a box with dress-up items, such as clothes, jewelry, shoes, crowns, and hats.

Invite a toddler to dress up with the clothes and accessories you have. As the toddler dresses up, say: "In the Bible, it talks about how God gives us many fine things. The people of the Bible dressed up and wore fancy jewelry. What are you going to wear?"

Affirm the choices the toddler makes, even if the clothes don't match or there are more accessories than clothes. The point is for the toddler to enjoy dressing up.

Consider using accessories yourself and tying what you wear to Bible stories:

• Wear a crown on your head to look like one of the queens or kings in the Bible.

• Place a blanket or sheet over your hair to look like a shepherd.

• Cradle a doll while talking about all the moms and dads in the Bible.

End the game by saying: "Let's thank God for giving us so many fun things to wear." Pray a short prayer with the toddler, such as: "Thank you, God, for all these great clothes! Amen."

Bonus Idea

Ask for dress-up donations from church members and watch sales—especially after Halloween when costumes often are marked down by 75 to 90 percent.

Stop and Help
Scripture: Luke 10:25-37

This Game Teaches: Help those who are sick or hurt, like the good Samaritan.

Supervision Tip: Monitor toddlers as they use a wagon or laundry basket.

Materials: One cardboard box, a red marker, a wagon or laundry basket, stuffed animals

Game: Before you play the game, place a red cross on an upside down cardboard box. Tell the toddler that this is the hospital. On the opposite side of the room, set up a wagon or a laundry basket. Place stuffed animals around the room.

Say: "This is our ambulance." Point to the wagon or laundry basket. Ask the toddler if he or she knows what an ambulance is. If the toddler doesn't know, tell what the ambulance is and demonstrate how an ambulance goes. (Emphasize that an ambulance moves, not that it goes fast so that you can prevent the toddler from possible accidents.)

Say: "We have sick and hurt animals around the room. Can you pick them up with your ambulance and bring them to the hospital over there?" Point to the box with the red cross on it.

Play the game with the toddler. (You may need to help the toddler at first since this is a rather complex game for a toddler to understand at first. Once the toddler knows what to do, the toddler usually really enjoys this game.)

Play the game a few times. Toddlers enjoy picking up the animals in the ambulance, bringing them to the hospital, and helping them get well at the hospital.

End the game by saying: "In the Bible, the good Samaritan helped someone who was hurt. You helped the sick and hurt animals. You picked them up in your ambulance and brought them to the hospital."

48

A Noisy Ark
Scripture: Genesis 7

This Game Teaches: There were a lot of different noisy animals on the ark.

Supervision Tip: Make eye contact with toddlers and enjoy the animal noises they make.

Materials: None

Game: Say: "In the Bible, the ark was filled with all the animals in the world. How many animals do you know?"

Make the sound of the following animals (one at a time) and see if the toddler can identify them:

- Dog (bark)
- Cow (moo)
- Duck (quack)
- Lion (roar)
- Cat (meow)
- Sheep (baa)
- Rooster (cock-a-doodle-doo)
- Horse (neigh)
- Pig (oink)
- Hen (cluck)

Then switch the game. Name the animal and see if the toddler can make the animal sound.

End the game by saying: "The animals made a lot of noise on the ark in the Bible. You know a lot of animals and the sounds they make."

Step by Step
Scripture: 1 Peter 2:21-25

This Game Teaches: Follow in Christ's steps.

Supervision Tip: Secure footprint papers to the floor so toddlers don't slip.

Materials: Paper, markers, masking tape, optional: access to a photocopier

Game: Before you play the game, trace one right foot and one left foot of a toddler. If you have access to a photocopier, make about fifteen copies of each one. Tape the footprints to the floor with a right foot next to a left foot, the footsteps close enough together so that a toddler can easily walk on the papers. (If you don't have access to a photocopier, cut out the left foot and the right foot and trace the feet onto paper.)

Once the footprint papers are secured to the floor, say to a toddler: "At church we learn about following Jesus. In the Bible, it says we should follow in Christ's steps." Encourage the toddler to start at one end of the papers secured to the floor and to match up his or her feet to the right foot and the left foot. Have the toddler move to the next set of footprints when you say one of these things:

• Jesus wants us to follow him. (The toddler moves to the next set of footprints.)

• Jesus likes it when we take steps in the right direction. (The toddler moves to the next set of footprints.)

• Walking with Jesus takes us on the right path. (The toddler moves to the next set of footprints.)

• Jesus knows the way to go. (The toddler moves to the next set of footprints.)

• Each step we take counts. (The toddler moves to the next set of footprints.)

End the game by saying: "We can follow in Christ's steps by coming to church and learning more about Jesus."

50

Bonus Tip

Use packing tape to create extra firm, nonslip surfaces for toddlers to walk on. Office and school supply stores sell packing tape that is clear, easily revealing the picture underneath it.

David and Goliath
Scripture: 1 Samuel 17

This Game Teaches: The difference between big and little.
Supervision Tip: Monitor toddlers' enthusiasm for the game. Play as long as they enjoy it.
Materials: Two pieces of paper, marker
Game: On one piece of paper, write the word *big*. On the other piece of paper, write the word *little*. Say: "In the Bible, Goliath was big and David was little. Let's walk around the room and find big things. What do you see?"

Walk with the child. Write the names of the items that the toddler says are big, such as table, crib (if the toddlers share a room with infants), and chair. When you finish, use the other sheet and look for items that are small, such as ball, stuffed animal, and pencil.

Then say: "When I call out the word big, walk over to something that's big and point to it. Okay?" Say the word big.

Then say the word little. Do this a few times, alternating big and little (or doing two of the same word in a row). This gives a toddler a fun way to learn the difference between big and little.

End the game by saying: "You know what's big and what's little. In the Bible, little David met up with big Goliath."

51

Happy and Sad, Good and Bad

Scripture: Mark 10:17-31

This Game Teaches: There are good and bad ways to act like Christians.

Supervision Tip: Supervise toddlers so they don't put the spoons into their mouths.

Materials: One white plastic spoon, a permanent black marker

Game: Before you play this game, draw a happy face on one side of the spoon (in the widest part that's shaped like a head). Draw a sad face on the other side. Simple drawings tend to work best.

Invite a toddler to play with you. Hold up the happy face side of the spoon. Say: "I'm so happy. This is a happy face." Turn the spoon over. Say: "I'm so sad. This is a sad face."

Ask the toddler to identify the faces as you show him or her the two faces one at a time again. Give the toddler the spoon. Say: "I'm going to tell you different ways that we can act. When I say one thing, you choose whether it's good (by showing the happy face of the spoon) or bad (by showing the sad face of the spoon). Ready?"

Say actions such as these:

- Listen to mom and dad
- Hit someone
- Help others
- Share
- Hurt someone
- Yell
- Smile
- Take a toy from someone else
- Go to church

End the game by saying: "The Bible tells us good and bad ways to act. You know a lot about good and bad ways to act. I'm so proud of you."

52

Your Sacred Name
Scripture: Psalm 139:13-16

53

This Game Teaches: God knows us now and even before we were born.

Supervision Tip: Keep track of where you hide the name cards so that toddlers don't become overly frustrated when they can't find them.

Materials: Six index cards for each toddler, a black marker

Game: Before you play the game, write one toddler's name one time on each of the six index cards. While the toddler is doing something else, keep one card and hide the other five around the room. Be sure that most of the card is visible so that the toddler can easily find the cards.

Ask the child named on the card to play. Show the toddler the one card with his or her name on it. Say: "This is your name. I love your name. Can you find five more of these cards with your name written on them? They're hidden around the room."

Walk around the room with the toddler as he or she searches for the cards. Affirm the toddler each time the toddler finds a card. Give clues if the toddler has trouble finding a card or two.

End the game by saying: "I love your name. God knows your name, and God even knew you before you were born."

Bonus Tip

To add another dimension to the game, use index cards in different colors. In addition to talking about the child's name, talk about the colors of the index cards.

Load Up the Baskets
Scripture: John 6:1-15

This Game Teaches: Miracles occur.

Supervision Tip: Keep other children safe by setting up the game away from other children.

Materials: A laundry basket, a bunch of wadded-up socks (where the pairs are placed together and turned inside out to form a small ball)

Game: Set up a laundry basket on the floor away from other children. Place a bunch of wadded-up socks about one foot away from the laundry basket. Ask a toddler to join you near the pile of socks.

54

Say, "Let's play a game. When Jesus fed the five thousand, he asked people to gather up all the leftovers when they were finished eating. We're going to pretend that these are leftover pieces of food." Hold up a sock ball.

Toss the sock ball into the laundry basket. Say, "Now it's your turn. Throw this into the basket."

Applaud the toddler's attempt, even if he or she misses. Encourage the toddler to try again. (Adjust the distance of where the toddler is standing, if needed.)

Encourage the toddler to continue throwing the sock balls until all of them are in the basket. Some toddlers may even want to do this again.

End the game by saying, "You got all these balls in the basket. You gathered up all the balls, just like the people in the Bible put all the extra food in their baskets after Jesus fed the five thousand."

Shake and Sing
Scripture: Exodus 15:1-21

This Game Teaches: Moses, Miriam, and the Israelites praised God after crossing the Red Sea.

Supervision Tip: Secure the bags so the rice or beans inside don't slip out.

Materials: Two lunch-size paper bags per toddler, washable markers, beans or rice, rubber bands

Game: Give a toddler two lunch-size paper bags and some washable markers. Encourage the toddler to decorate the bags.

Once the toddler finishes, partially fill each bag with beans or rice. Close the bags tightly with rubber bands.

Show the toddler how to shake the bags to make them rattle. Encourage the toddler to hold a bag in each hand and shake them at the same time and then try shaking them one at a time, alternating the shaking for a different sound.

Say: "In the Bible, Moses and his people sang and praised God. I'll sing and you can praise God by jumping around and shaking your bags."

Sing this song to the tune of "If You're Happy and You Know It":

If you're happy and you know it, shake your bag (shake, shake)
If you're happy and you know it, shake your bag (shake, shake)
If you're happy and you know it, then we'll shake to surely show it
If you're happy and you know it, shake your bag (shake, shake).

End the game by saying: "I'm glad we praised God by singing and shaking our bags. God likes it when we sing and praise God."

Bonus Idea

To add more music to the praising, sew some jingle bells onto elastic that will fit a toddler's ankles. Toddlers love to jump, stomp, and run to make the jingle bells ring.

55

Two-by-Two Shoes
Scripture: Acts 7:30-34

This Game Teaches: Moses took off his sandals to stand on holy ground.

Supervision Tip: Choose pairs of shoes that don't have sharp edges or tears.

Materials: Three to four pairs of shoes (ideally choose pairs that are radically different in color and size, such as a pair of brown sandals, a pair of tall black boots, a white pair of tennis shoes, a brown pair of men's shoes, a blue pair of children's shoes, a pink pair of fuzzy slippers, a pair of baby shoes)

Game: In front of a toddler, set up a line of shoes that are not in their pairs. If possible, include one pair of sandals. Say, "In the Bible, people sometimes took off their shoes when they talk to God on holy ground. Here are some shoes, but they're mixed up. Each one has a partner. Can you find the partner?"

Learning to classify, sort, and find patterns are essential skills for toddlers to learn, and they love doing these types of games, as long as they're not too easy or too hard.

As the child finds a match, talk about whom the shoe possibly belongs to and why the person would wear it. For example, "Those fuzzy slippers belong to Jeannette. She wears them when she puts on her pajamas and gets ready for bed," or "Luis wears these boots when it snows outside. The boots keep his feet warm and dry."

When the child finds the sandal pair, say: "In the Bible, people like Moses wore sandals. They lived in a hot, dry, sandy climate, which is like summer."

End the game by saying, "You found all the pairs of shoes! If Moses were here, he could easily find his sandals, thanks to you."

56

Beautiful Minds
Scripture: Daniel 5:10-17

This Game Teaches: Daniel used his incredible mind to make good choices.

Supervision Tip: Spend time with the toddler during the game and enjoy being together.

Materials: Pieces of paper, washable markers

Game: Ask a toddler to sit next to you. On one of the pieces of paper, write: X O X O X. Give the toddler a marker. Ask: "What comes next: X or O?"

If the toddler has never done a pattern game before, he or she may need your help. (Point out the pattern and how it repeats without giving away the answer.) If the toddler figures it out, go on to another pattern. If not, show the toddler what comes next and try again.

Always use patterns of two. Other patterns to try include:

• A B A B A
• Happy face, sad face, happy face, sad face, happy face
• 1 0 1 0 1
• Yellow scribble, blue scribble, yellow scribble, blue scribble, yellow scribble

End the game by saying: "In the Bible, Daniel used his mind to make smart choices. I'm happy when you think hard to figure out these patterns."

57

96

Your Church, My Church
Scripture: 1 Timothy 2

This Game Teaches: It's important for Christians to come together to worship.

Supervision Tip: Periodically check this handmade book to see if any repairs are needed.

Materials: 8 1/2 x 11 inch construction paper, glue, a camera and film, a stapler, a marker

Game: Create a handmade book of church photos before you play this game. Take photos of the outside of your church, the room you're in with toddlers, the pastor, regular caregivers for toddlers, the altar, the pulpit, the sanctuary, and other important places, people, and symbols of your church. Glue one picture onto one piece of construction paper. Continue to glue pictures on separate pieces of construction paper until you have glued all the photos. Place the page with the picture of the outside of your church on top. Staple the construction paper pieces together into a book format. Label the cover "Our Church."

Have a toddler sit in your lap. Give the toddler the book. Say: "Look! This is a book about our church. See! This is a picture of our church. We're inside that building right now."

Encourage the toddler to open the pages carefully. Talk about each picture, asking the toddler questions. If you have a picture of a caregiver who is nearby, ask the toddler if he or she can find that person in the room.

After you've looked at the book together, start at the beginning of the book again. Have the toddler do an action after each page. Actions might include:

- Clapping
- Jumping up and stomping your feet
- Running around the room
- Shouting "Alleluia" and then whispering it

58

End the game by saying: "God made the day with the blue sky. (Pause for the toddler to act.) God also made the nighttime sky. (Pause.) I'm glad that God made both daytime and nighttime."

Peek-a-Boo! Who Loves You?
Scripture: John 3:16

This Game Teaches: God loves us and we love each other.
Supervision Tip: Encourage toddlers to hug gently.
Materials: None
Game: Ask a toddler to play with you. Say: "I'm going to name a person in this room who loves you. When I say that person's name, go up to that person and hug him or her."

Practice this part of the game. For example, say: "Peek-a-Boo! Who loves you? I see that Liza (name of a caregiver in the room) loves you." Encourage Liza and the toddler to hug.

Play the game by naming other adults and toddlers in the room, one at a time. Each time you do this, say: "Peek-a-Boo! Who loves you? I see that (name of person) loves you."

End the game by saying: "God loves you very much, just like I love you." Hug the toddler.

Bonus Idea

Create a bulletin board with this love theme. Cut hearts out of red construction paper and place a photograph of each child and each caregiver in a separate heart. If you wish, you also could add parents and your pastor. With infants, play the game by placing small cloths over the top of each heart and lifting the cloth to see who is underneath it.

60

Fun Games for
YOUNG PRESCHOOLERS
(FROM 3 TO 4 YEARS)

The biggest change when children become young preschoolers is that they begin to play with other children. At first, however, their playtime will vacillate between parallel play and cooperative play. Because of this shift, the most effective play occurs with four or fewer young preschoolers with one adult. The absolute ideal is two young preschoolers with one adult.

Even in small groups, preschoolers will move in and out of interaction with their peers, switching to a solitary action before joining in group play again. By the time children turn three and a half, they're more adept at playing for longer periods with another child or a small group of children.

Young preschoolers embrace play that involves action. They love to run, jump, and move in different ways. Many have a lot of energy, and games can help channel that energy. Sometimes when preschoolers begin to act up, the best response is to play a physical game that gets them to move.

In playing games that teach about Bible stories, emphasize the concrete. When young preschoolers see a fish, they think of a fish, not a symbol of Christianity. (And no amount of teaching will convince them otherwise.) Games that allow children to experience what Bible characters faced or felt often will be most effective. They'll talk about what it felt like to be confused and lost when they play "From Here to There" on page 117 and how many animals there are in "All Mine" on page 114, just like they'll long remember the story of Jesus washing the disciples' feet if young preschoolers actually take off their socks and shoes and have an adult immerse their feet in water.

All Our Friends
Scripture: John 15:11-17

This Game Teaches: Love one another; make and keep friends.
Supervision Tip: Monitor children as they gently toss the beanbag.
Materials: A beanbag (or small, sturdy stuffed animal)
Game: Have children sit in a circle. Give one child a beanbag (or a small, sturdy stuffed animal). Tell the child to say his or her own name before saying "is a friend." The child then gently tosses the beanbag to another child in the circle. That child catches the beanbag, says his or her name before saying "is a friend," and tosses the beanbag to another child. For example, if Luis gets the beanbag first, he says, "Luis is a friend" and tosses it to Ashley who says, "Ashley is a friend" before tossing it to another child.

After playing the game for a short while, say, "Each one of us is a friend. Now we're going to play the game a little bit differently. Instead of saying your name, say the name of the child you're tossing the beanbag to." For example if Teresa gets the beanbag first, she says, "Mike is a friend" before tossing the beanbag to Mike.

End the game by saying, "In the Bible it says to love one another and be friends. Our church is full of friends and people who love each other."

61

Hip Hooray!
Scripture: Exodus 23:14-19

This Game Teaches: It's important to celebrate when we're happy.

Supervision Tip: Ensure that noisemakers don't break and spill their contents.

Materials: A shakable noisemaker for each child, such as a rattle, a preschool instrument, or a securely fastened empty film canister with dried beans inside

Game: Say: "The Bible had many times when there were parties. In the book of Exodus, there were three big parties that the people had every year." Give each child a noisemaker. Say: "When I say the word celebrate, shake your instruments and dance around the room. When I say stop, stop and be still until I say celebrate again."

Do the game once. Then sing this song to the tune of "Hickory Dickory Dock":

Here we go dancing again
We're glad to say, amen.
We jumped to say
A hip hooray
Here we go dancing again!

Repeat the game again. This time have children stay in place as you ask them to shake their instruments in different ways: holding instruments up high, holding them down low, shaking fast, shaking slow, clapping their hands together (with the shaker still in their hands), and shaking their whole bodies.

End the game by saying: "The people in the Bible celebrated because they were happy. It is good to celebrate the good things that God gives us."

62

Happy Helpers
Scripture:
Matthew 25:34-40

This Game Teaches: God calls us to help others.

Supervision Tip: Keep the floor clear so that children don't slip or trip when they run.

Materials: Pictures (or photocopies) of children's handprints, masking tape

63

Game: Before you play this game, get pictures (or photocopies) of children's handprints. (Some craft and educational stores may also sell these in packages of die cuts. If you're going to make them, draw around one hand of a child and make many photocopies of the hand. You don't need to cut out the hands.)

Bring the children together to play the game. Walk over to the sink (if your room has one). Say: "This is a helping station. How do the sink and the water help us?" Encourage children to talk about washing their hands. Place a piece of masking tape on one of the hand prints and ask one of the children to hang up the sign near the sink.

Visit other areas of the room, and repeat the process. Include areas such as these:

- the toy chest or toy area (for picking up toys)
- light switch (for turning off and on the lights)
- snack table (for helping with snack set up and clean up)
- coat rack (for hanging up coats)
- art area (for putting away markers and paper)

Hang up one hand at each area.

Then do a helping-hand tour. Have everyone go to the sink and help each other wash and dry their hands. Then go to the light switch. Have children take turns switching the light off and on. Go to the toy area and pick up toys, and so forth.

End the game by saying, "God wants us to be great helpers. The Bible says it's good to help each other."

A Safe Place
Scripture: 2 Kings 11

This Game Teaches: People care for us and keep us safe.

Supervision Tip: Encourage children to move slowly to keep the sheet on their backs and not pinch anybody's fingers or toes.

Materials: Bedsheet

Game: Have children huddle together on their hands and knees in an area far from chairs, tables, and other things to bump into. Say: "I'm going to place a large sheet over all of us. So be very still while I do this because it's going to get a bit dark." Kneel down with the children and place a sheet over the top of the entire group.

Say: "In the Bible, there was a baby who was going to grow up to be a king. His name was Prince Joash. The problem was that someone didn't want Joash to be king. That person wanted to hurt baby Joash. So Joash's aunt and uncle hid him, just like we're hiding under this sheet."

Encourage the children to be very quiet. Say, "I think someone is coming. Let's very slowly and quietly move over this way." Point with your finger the direction you intend to move. On hands and knees, slowly move while keeping the cloth on your back. Then stop.

"We're safe over here. Moms, dads, grandpas, grandmas, and all kinds of adults know how to keep us safe. Oh! Oh! Now listen! I think we have to move again." Point in another direction. With the children, slowly move on hands and knees.

End the game by saying, "Prince Joash had to stay in hiding for seven years. Can you imagine that? We just played a hiding game, but it was for only a few minutes. God and adults keep us safe from danger."

64

Beautiful Bodies
Scripture:
1 Corinthians 6:19-20

This Game Teaches: Our bodies are God's temples.

Supervision Tip: Have children spread out so they don't bump into each other.

Materials: None

65

Game: Have children stand up. Say: "God made our bodies so that they move and do lots of things. When we exercise and take care of our bodies, that makes God happy. Let's see how small we can make our bodies. Sit on the floor and curl up in a tight ball." Give children time to do this. When children finish, do these different exercises, one at a time:

• Stretch out as far as possible (stand up, spread legs apart, and lift arms high into the air)

• Run in place

• Stand and then touch your toes

• Sit down, lean back, and kick your feet in the air

• Stand and twist back and forth

• Sit and clap

• Stand up and have everyone hold hands and make a group circle

End the game by saying: "God likes it when we take good care of our bodies. We moved our bodies in a lot of ways and gave our bodies some good exercise."

More Than You Think

Scripture: Genesis 1

This Game Teaches: All the wonders of creation.

Supervision Tip: Play the game with six children or fewer to ensure they don't bump into each other. If you have more than six children, create more Xs on the floor.

Materials: Masking tape

Game: Before the game, create three large Xs on the floor, about two to three feet apart, with masking tape. (It's best if the Xs are not in a line.)

Have each child stand on a different X. (If you have more than three children playing, have up to two children standing on each X.)

Say: "When I tell you to go, run to another X on the floor. Make sure there are not more than two children on that X. There is room for everyone. Ready? Go."

Give children time to run. When they all get on an X, say: "God created many things. God created animals. I want each one of you to name one animal." Have each child name an animal. When everyone finishes, say "go" again and have the children move.

When all the children get on an X, name another category of creation, such as people (names of people they know), places (home, church, store, school), food, colors, and so forth. Have each child identify something specific in that category before you have them go again.

End the game by saying: "I'm glad that God created so many things. You named so many things that God created."

Heart to Heart
Scripture: 1 John 3:11-18

This Game Teaches: Love one another.

Supervision Tip: Clear a large area so children can play the game safely.

Materials: Red construction paper, markers, scissors, a lunch-size paper bag, paper clips

Game: Before the game, make hearts out of red construction paper. (Make each heart a different size.) Make half as many hearts as you have children. For example, if you usually have six children, you'll need three hearts. If you have twelve children, you'll need six hearts. Decorate each heart in a different way. Choose ideas such as these: stripes, stars, circles, zigzags, triangles, happy faces, cats, squares. Then cut each heart in half the long way so that each piece has a hump. (Keep each heart set together with paper clips.)

To play the game, count the number of children you have. If you have an odd number, ask an adult to play so that you have an even number of participants. Place half as many hearts into the bag as you have people. (If you have eight children, you need four hearts. If you have twenty children, you need ten hearts.) Remove all the paper clips and mix up the pieces.

Have each child randomly pick one heart piece out of the bag and not show it to anyone else. Once everyone has a heart piece, spread throughout the room. Say: "I'm going to sing a song while you walk around the room. As soon as I stop, hold out your heart piece so that other people can see it, and try to find your match."

Sing a song, any song you wish. As soon as you stop, watch the children find their partner. Then congratulate them. Have the children all place their pieces back into the bag. Mix up the pieces and play the game again.

End the game by saying: "The Bible teaches us to love one another. By finding our partners with our hearts, we found lots of people who love us."

67

Count the Stars
Scripture: Genesis 15:5

This Game Teaches: God tells Abram to count the stars.

Supervision Tip: Watch how children interact with each other as they play and keep them safe.

Materials: One piece of white paper, yellow photocopy paper, photocopier, marker, masking tape

Game: Before the game, draw a large star on a piece of 8 1/2 x 11 inch white paper. Using yellow photocopy paper, make twelve copies so that you have twelve stars. Number the stars with a large number from one to twelve so that each star has a different number. Hang the stars along a hallway the children use frequently. Place the stars in order and hang them so children can easily reach them.

Have children line up in the hallway near the star with the number one on it. Say: "In the Bible, God told Abram to count the stars. Together, let's count the stars. As we go by each star, tap it with your hand while you say the number." Lead the children down the hallway as they count (and tap) from one to twelve.

Line up again near the first star. Say: "Now we're going to take turns. When it's your turn, walk and tap each star as you count from one to twelve." Give children turns to do this. When everyone has finished, encourage children to do this again in a different way, such as: running, jumping, or holding another child's hand.

End the game by saying: "In the Bible, Abram counted the stars, just like you counted the stars. I'm so proud that you're learning your numbers and that you can count."

68

All the Money
Scripture: Mark 12:41-44

This Game Teaches: The widow gives all her money to God.

Supervision Tip: Keep younger children from picking up the coins and placing them in their mouths.

Materials: Two plastic bowls, a towel, a bunch of pennies, a bunch of silver coins (nickels, dimes, and quarters), clear adhesive tape

Game: Before the game, spread a towel on the floor. About two feet away, place two bowls. Tape a penny to the inside bottom of one bowl and tape a silver coin (a nickel or quarter are better, since they're larger than a dime) to the inside bottom of the other bowl. Cover the towel with pennies, nickels, dimes, and quarters.

Have the children line up along the towel. Say: "In the Bible, a woman put her coins in the offering plates and gave them to the church. We have two offering plates over there." Point to the bowls. "One holds brown coins called pennies." Show the children the bowl with the penny taped to the inside bottom. "The other holds silver coins, such as nickels, dimes, and quarters." Show the children the other bowl.

Say: "When I tell you to start, pick up one coin off this towel and walk over to the bowls. Put your coin in the bowl that matches your coin, either with the brown coins or the silver coins. When you're done, walk back to the towel and pick up a different coin and bring it to the right bowl. Keep doing this until all the coins are gone. There's no need to rush because we have lots of coins."

Start the game. At the end of the game, examine the bowls with the children and see what they think about what's inside. (Ensure that there are no pennies in the silver bowl and vice versa. If there are, see if the children have ideas of what should change.)

End the game by saying, "When we come to church, it's good to bring money to give to God, just like the widow did in the Bible."

69

All Mine
Scripture: Psalm 50:10

This Game Teaches: All animals are God's animals.

Supervision Tip: Repair any stuffed animals that may have loose parts.

Materials: A large number (and variety) of stuffed animals, a towel

Game: Before the game, spread the stuffed animals on the floor throughout the room. Place a towel in the middle of the room.

Say: "Let's play a game. Throughout the room are a bunch of stuffed animals. I'm going to name something about a stuffed animal, and I want you to look at each stuffed animal.

If the special thing I named is true about that stuffed animal, pick up the stuffed animal, bring it to the towel, and leave it there. If the stuffed animal doesn't have the special thing, look at a different stuffed animal."

Name a specific characteristic, such as black eyes. Wait until all the children have gathered the appropriate animals and placed them on the towel. Affirm them and have them carry the stuffed animals back into the playing area to play again.

Name other specific characteristics (depending on the stuffed animals you have):

- A tail
- Teeth
- Black fur
- Fins
- Teddy bear (if you have more than one of a specific animal)
- Ears
- Wings

End by saying "an animal you love." Encourage children to pick an animal they love and stand on the towel with the animal. Say: "Hug an animal and say mine, mine, mine." Give children time to do this. "All animals are God's animals. God loves all the animals, and we love animals too."

70

Colors Around Us
Scripture: Revelation 9:17

This Game Teaches: People are to be hopeful during hard times.

Supervision Tip: Prevent children from bumping each other during this game (since some children will pay more attention to looking at the floor than at each other).

Materials: Twelve pieces of construction paper (four blue, four red, and four yellow), masking tape

Game: Before the game, create one big circle on the floor with the construction paper (mixing up the three colors throughout the circle). Secure the construction paper to the floor with masking tape.

Have children stand in the middle of the circle with the colors surrounding them. Say: "Colors remind us to be happy. In the Bible, people talked about colors when life was hard to remind everyone that there also are good things. When I name a color, walk over to that color in the circle and place one foot on that color. Note that there is more than one choice. If I say red, for example, there are red squares here, here, here, and here." Point out the four places where the red papers are.

Start the game. First name yellow, then blue, then red, giving children time to find the color and place one foot on it. Once children get the hang of the game, you can do it faster and encourage them to run.

End the game by saying: "God made all these beautiful colors to remind us to be happy. As you grow, you will learn more and more colors. I'm proud of how you're beginning to learn the names of colors."

71

Bonus Idea

Consider playing this game with shapes (use a square, a circle, and a triangle), numbers (use 1, 2, 3), or alphabet letters (use A, B, C). Young preschoolers are just beginning to learn these basics, and this game makes the learning fun.

From Here to There
Scripture: Exodus

This Game Teaches: Moses led the people from Egypt (where they were slaves) to freedom in the promised land.

Supervision Tip: Play the game with three or fewer children at a time to ensure their safety.

Materials: Ten paper plates, masking tape, marker

Game: Before the game, label each paper plate from one to ten with the marker. Tape the plates to the floor randomly (so that they do not go in order from one to ten).

Say: "In the Bible, Moses led the people from Egypt to the promised land. This didn't happen fast. It took years and years, and the path wasn't always clear. We're now going to play a game where we are the people trying to find our way to the promised land."

Start by saying the number one. Have the children look for that number and then place one part of their foot on the plate. When everyone has found it, say the number two. Continue until the children reach ten. (This should look like a preschool-size dot-to-dot picture since the numbers are not in order.) Help any child who has trouble with numbers. Part of the point of the game is to teach numbers in addition to the Bible stories.

If the children enjoyed the game, play it again. If the children know their numbers well, count backward from ten to one.

End the game by saying: "It takes a long time to get from one place to another when the path is not clear. That's what it was like for the people during the Exodus. They trusted God to lead the way, and they made it to the promised land."

72

Hand to Hand
Scripture:
1 Corinthians 12:12-31

This Game Teaches: Every part of the body is important.

Supervision Tip: Encourage children to be gentle with each other as they play.

Materials: None

73

Game: Have each child find a partner. If you have an odd number of children, have an adult join in to be that child's partner.

Say: "God made our wonderful bodies, and each part of our body is special. Face your partner. When I name a body part, I want you to touch your partner's body part with that part of your body. Ready?"

Name these body parts (one at a time):

* Hand
* Foot
* Arm
* Leg
* Finger
* Elbow (this might be a part children don't know well)
* Bellies (this usually causes a lot of laughter)

End the game by saying: "Every part of our bodies is wonderful. Let's use our hands to clap for God." (Clap.)

Nesting Birds

Scripture: Psalm 104:12

This Game Teaches: Birds make their nests and sing.

Supervision Tip: Clear a large area so children can run around the room.

Materials: None

Game: Sit on the floor with your legs crossed and have several adults sit on the floor with their legs crossed, too. Encourage each child to sit in the lap of an adult. (You may need to play this game a few times if you have more children than adults. For each time you play, have the same number of children and adults.)

Say: "Look at all the little birds we have, and they're each sitting in a nest. What sound do little birds make?" Encourage the children to tweet like birds. Say: "The wind is blowing gently through the trees. The little birds love to rock back and forth." Begin slowly rocking back and forth while cradling the child in your lap. Encourage the other adults to do the same.

Say: "Suddenly, a big gust of wind comes and knocks the nest over. The little birds must fly out of the nests and fly around the sky." Gently tumble the child out of your lap and stand up so that the child must leave. Encourage children to run around the room, flapping their arms like wings and tweeting like birds.

After some time has passed, sit down and cross your legs. Encourage the others adults to sit, too. Say: "The little birds see that there are new nests. Can they find a different nest than the one they nestled in before?" The children climb into another adult's lap.

Repeat the game again with the gentle rocking and then the nest tumbling over.

End the game by saying: "The Bible tells about birds making their nests and singing. God cares for all the birds, animals, and people in the world."

74

Walk and Praise
Scripture: Romans 15:7-13

This Game Teaches: Paul says to praise Christ.

Supervision Tip: Monitor children so they don't bump into each other during the game.

Materials: A large picture of Jesus (at least 8 1/2 x 11 inch), masking tape

Game: Before the game, tape a picture of Jesus to the floor with masking tape. (Ask your Christian education director or pastor for a picture. Otherwise Christian bookstores, Christian online stores, and denominations' supply stores will have a picture you can purchase.)

Show children the picture of Jesus on the floor. Briefly talk about who Jesus is. (For example, Jesus is God's son. Jesus healed people. Jesus told everyone to follow God. Jesus came and died for our sins.) Explain that we love Jesus and we follow Jesus.

Have children form a circle around the picture of Jesus on the floor. Have children walk around the picture. As they do so, encourage them to sing with you to the tune of "London Bridge Is Falling Down":

(Verse 1)
Walk around our Jesus Christ
Jesus Christ, Jesus Christ
Walk around our Jesus Christ
We all love him.

(Verse 2)
Clap now for our Jesus Christ (clap)
Jesus Christ, Jesus Christ
Clap now for our Jesus Christ (clap)
Clap for Jesus (clap a bunch of times).

End the game by saying: "The Bible says it's good to praise Jesus Christ. We praised Jesus Christ by clapping. Let's clap one more time for Jesus." (Clap.)

75

A Time for Everything
Scripture: Ecclesiastes 3:1-8

This Game Teaches: There is a time for everything.

Supervision Tip: Monitor children to prevent them from bumping heads as they look at the floor during this game.

Materials: Twelve paper plates, marker, masking tape

Game: Before the game, use the marker to draw a clock face on each paper plate. Draw one o'clock on one, two o'clock on another, and so forth until you get to twelve o'clock. Tape the clock face paper plates onto the floor, making a line from one o'clock to twelve o'clock.

Say: "The Bible says that there is a time for everything (Ecclesiastes 3:1-8). Every day we have time to do lots of things. Let's start at seven o'clock. Where's seven o'clock?" Give children time to search for seven o'clock. Ask: "What do you do first thing in the morning?" Give children time to talk about waking up, eating breakfast, getting dressed, and so on.

Ask: "Where's ten o'clock?" Give children time to find that clock. Talk about how you read a clock face if some children are struggling. Ask: "What do you do in the morning before lunch?" Some kids go to preschool classes, others take naps, some watch TV, some help their parents with household tasks.

Continue with other times, such as twelve o'clock noon (lunchtime), three o'clock (playtime, nap time), six o'clock (dinnertime), eight o'clock (bedtime). Then ask children what else they do in their day. When a child names something, name a time when that might happen and have children find the clock. Repeat for a number of different named activities.

End the game by saying: "There's a time for everything. There's a time for waking up and going to sleep, eating breakfast and eating dinner, playing and taking naps."

76

Every Step Counts
Scripture: Proverbs 4:20-27

This Game Teaches: Walk in God's way.

Supervision Tip: Encourage children to keep their hands to themselves.

Materials: Masking tape (or chalk if you wish to do this outside)

Game: Before the game, create a wavy line with masking tape on the floor (or with chalk outside on a sidewalk or concrete play area).

Have children stand in line at one end of the line. Say: "God wants us to walk along God's path. Let's walk along this path and see how we do."

Ask the children to first walk along the wavy path from one end to the other end. When they get to the other end, have them move along the path in one of these ways:

- Tiptoe
- Giant steps
- Running
- Heel to toe
- Little steps

Continue to move back and forth along the line, using different types of movement.

End the game by saying: "The Bible says it's good for us to walk in God's path. You walked along this path in a lot of different ways, and you were great at keeping on each part of the path, even when it moved in a different direction."

77

Jailed, Then Free!
Scripture: Acts 16

This Game Teaches: Paul and Silas were freed from jail by an earthquake.

Supervision Tip: Be aware that some children may not like the sensation of having masking tape on their pants or legs.

Materials: A few rolls of masking tape and extra adult help, if possible

Game: Have children spread throughout the room and sit on the floor. Say: "We're going to play a Bible game about Paul and Silas. Paul and Silas loved to tell people about Jesus because they loved Jesus so much. But not everyone wanted to hear what they had to say, so some people threw Paul and Silas in jail. We're going to pretend to be Paul and Silas."

Give each adult a roll of masking tape. Go around from child to child and tape their legs to the floor. (Use just one piece of masking tape across each leg.) Encourage the children to sit still and imagine what it must be like to be in chains in jail where they can't be free. Tell the children more about what it's like to be in jail (you can't go where you want to go, you live in a small cell, you can't be with your family and friends, etc.) as you place masking tape on each child's legs.

When you're finished, say: "Paul and Silas sat in jail, but they didn't complain. Instead they sang songs." Lead the children in a song they know, such as "Jesus Loves Me," "Jesus Loves the Little Children," or "The B-I-B-L-E." Sing the song once. Then say: "Then a big earthquake came and loosened everyone's chains. Everyone move your legs up and down until your masking tape breaks." (Children really enjoy this part.) Once everyone is free, have the children jump and say, "I'm free! I'm free! I'm free! I'm free!"

End the game by saying: "In the Bible, Paul and Silas were in jail, but a big earthquake came and set them free from their chains. Once they were out of jail, they praised God for being with them."

78

A Wild Wind
Scripture: Psalm 104

This Game Teaches: God made the wind and the air.

Supervision Tip: Prevent young children from picking up the deflated balloon and putting it into their mouths.

Materials: A couple of balloons

Game: Take out one balloon and place the other balloons in a secure place so that children cannot get them.

Say: "It takes wind and air to inflate a balloon. I'm going to fill this balloon full of air. When I let go of the end, it will race across the room as the air goes out of it. Chase the balloon and pick it up when it falls to the floor. Then bring it back to me."

Demonstrate the game. (You do not tie the end of the balloon, just hold it until you let it go.) Then play the game. Before you release the end of the balloon, however, sing this song to the tune of "Row, Row, Row Your Boat":

Let's blow it up with air
'Till it's nice and round (then release the full balloon)
Chase it now, chase it now
Pick it off the ground

Repeat the game a few times. Then end the game by saying: "God made the wind and the air, which is what we used in this balloon. We have an awesome God."

Manna, Manna Everywhere
Scripture: Numbers 11:7-9

This Game Teaches: Israelites picked up manna from the ground.

Supervision Tip: Prevent younger children from putting cotton balls into their mouths.

Materials: A large bag of cotton balls

Game: Say: "In the Bible there was a time when food called manna fell from the sky during the night while the people slept. Then the people woke up and picked up the manna for the day."

Have the children lie on the floor. If possible, turn off the lights. Say: "We're pretending that we live in Bible times. It's nighttime, and we're pretending to sleep. Close your eyes." Some children will close their eyes. Others won't. That's okay. Motion for the ones who don't close their eyes not to make any noise as you drop cotton balls all around the children. (Use the whole bag so that there are a lot of cotton balls.)

Turn on the lights. Say: "Good morning! Let's all wake up and open our eyes. Stretch and get up. Oh! What's this! These look like manna from heaven. How many can you pick up and hold?" Encourage children to pick up all the cotton balls. As they do so, say this rhyme:

Manna, manna
Everywhere
Manna, manna
Fell from the air
Manna, manna
On the ground
Manna, manna
To be found

End the game by saying: "God took care of the people in Bible times just like God cares for us now. I had fun playing this game .about manna, the food that fell from heaven."

Fun Games for
OLDER PRESCHOOLERS
(FROM 4 TO 5 YEARS)

Their expanding vocabulary, their enthusiasm, and their willingness to try new things all add up to interesting playtimes with older preschoolers. Their muscles ache to move, and they relish games that open up new worlds to them.

Adults also enjoy playing with children at this age because older preschoolers begin to articulate heart-warming thoughts about God. "I just love God for making babies," a child said after the birth of her brother. "Someday I just want to meet God and say thank you for my great life," another said. Older preschoolers also ask interesting questions, such as where heaven is, what God looks like, and why God made smelly garbage. Since older preschoolers still are in the first stage of spiritual development, it's essential that we allow children to ask questions, learn more faith stories, and experience faith rituals that give life meaning. Older preschoolers cannot often discern between fantasy and reality, so their faith is often a mix of their concrete experience and observations along with their great imagination.

Keep games highly sensory and try to engage children's sense of sight, hearing, touch, smell, and taste as often as possible. Since older preschoolers are more adept at playing in groups, you can experiment with different group sizes. (Although you'll quickly find the point where a group requires chaos control.) Still, part of the fun is letting older preschoolers experience what it's like to play a game with a couple of children versus a larger group. As long as games are simple, concrete, and interesting, most older preschoolers are willing to try something new, and many will even come up with solutions of how to take a game in another creative direction.

Who Me?
Scripture: Acts 9:1-19

This Game Teaches: It's important to follow God.

Supervision Tip: Shine the light in the direction of children, but not into their eyes.

Materials: A flashlight

Game: Demonstrate how to play this game. Say: "In the Bible, God wanted a man named Saul to follow him. So God shone a bright light on Saul and called out his name. We're going to play a game. We're all going to walk around the room. When I shine the flashlight on you and say your name, sit down, close your eyes, and say, 'Who me? I can't see!' Then you may peek between your fingers to watch the other children get called one by one."

Begin to play the game. Call out the name of the child as you turn on the flashlight in his or her direction. Say, "There is (name of child). You can no longer walk or see." Wait while the child sits down and closes his or her eyes. You may need to help the first few children until they catch on to the game. Then continue the game until you have called out all the children and had them sit.

End the game by saying, "Now you can see! Now you can walk! Stand up and follow me!" Have the children stand up and form a line behind you. Then lead them around the room. Say: "Saul followed God, just like you're following me. It's good when we all follow God."

81

Wrists of Wonder
Scripture: Genesis 1

This Game Teaches: The wonders of God's creation are all around us.

Supervision Tip: Watch what children pick up since some discoveries aren't so wonderful.

Materials: Masking tape, access to the outdoors

Game: Take children outside on a comfortable day. Tie a piece of masking tape (sticky side out) around each child's wrist. Say: "God made many wonderful things. As we walk, look around and pick up pretty parts of God's creation and stick them onto your bracelets. By the end of our walk, you will have a wrist of wonder."

Take the children on a walk. Monitor what children pick up, and give them ideas if they're having trouble. (Great items to add to these bracelets are grass, leaves, and seeds.)

As you collect items, sing this song to the tune of "Row, Row, Row Your Boat":

(Verse 1)
Look, look, look around
What can you now find?
Lots of things, lots of things, lots of things, lots of things
Isn't our God kind?

(Verse 2)
Pick, pick, pick things up
What is in your fist?
Lots of things, lots of things, lots of things, lots of things
Stick them to your wrist

After the bracelets are full, have children stand in a circle. Ask them to raise the arm that has the bracelet. Have children put that arm in the middle of the circle, their extended hands all touching. Have them walk in the circle and together say, "Thank you, God, for making so many wonderful wonders."

End the game by saying: "God created many beautiful things on our earth. We now have bracelets to remind us of God's creation."

82

Pictures of Thankfulness

Scripture:
1 Thessalonians 5:16-18

83

This Game Teaches: God gives us a lot to be thankful for.

Supervision Tip: Clear the area around the circle so that children don't slip.

Materials: A piece of white paper for each child, crayons, masking tape

Game: Give each child a piece of paper and some crayons. Say: "God gives us a lot of things to be thankful for. Draw a picture of something you're glad you have. It might be a person in your family, a pet, a toy, something in your home." Give children time to draw and color their pictures. Draw one so that you can start the game.

When they finish, ask children to bring their pictures with them and sit in a circle with you. Say: "I'm going to start the game. Here's how we play. I'm going to stand up with my picture in the middle of the circle. I'm going to tell you what I drew and why I am so thankful for it. I'll slowly turn around in the circle so everyone can see the picture. Then together, we'll raise one arm in the air and shout 'Hooray (say your name). Hooray (the object you drew). Hooray God!' "

Stand in the middle of the circle, describe your picture, say why you're thankful for it, slowly turn around in the circle, and then lead the children in saying: "Hooray (your name). Hooray (the object you drew). Hooray God!"

Then have the child sitting to your left go next. It will take awhile for children to remember the sequence of events, so guide them through it until they catch on.

End the game after every child has participated. Hang all the pictures on one wall. Say: "Let's shout hooray three times for all the great things God gives us."

Love from Here to There
Scripture:
Deuteronomy 11:8-32

This Game Teaches: Love is all around us.

Supervision Tip: Watch carefully and remove balloons immediately after they pop.

Materials: Red, round balloons

Game: Inflate a balloon and tie the end. Have children take off their socks and shoes and place them far from the playing area. (Remove your socks and shoes, too.) Sit in a circle with the children.

Say: "Love is all around us. God loves us. We love God. People love us. We love other people. I have a red balloon. I think of it as the love balloon. We're going to pass this red balloon around the circle to show how love goes all around." Pass the balloon to the child next to you and encourage children to pass the balloon around the circle until it comes back to you.

Have everyone in the circle back up so that there is more space between each person. (Ideally you want to have enough space between each child so that another child could actually fit in the empty space.) Then say: "Now we're going to pass the balloon around with only our feet. Ready?" Place the balloon between your two bare feet. Lean back and balance yourself with your hands while you hold your feet and the balloon in the air. Pivot slowly to the child next to you. (This is why you want enough space between children.) Use your feet to pass the balloon to the feet of the child next to you. Do this slowly since this requires balance and eye-foot coordination. Children will enjoy this challenge, and this game often brings out the giggles.

End the game once the balloon has made it around the circle. Say:

84

"Love is all around. From our toes to our head and from here to there, love is all around."

Another Way Home
Scripture: Matthew 2:1-12

This Game Teaches: The wise men go home another way to keep Jesus safe.

Supervision Tip: Monitor children since they can become entangled in the elastic.

Materials: Lots of elastic (available at fabric stores), scissors

Game: Stretch elastic around chairs, tables, and other pieces of furniture in your room. (Ideally have elastic at different heights to make this game more challenging and fun, but keep it between one and two feet off the ground.)

Say: "The three wise men visited Baby Jesus. They went home a different way because they heard that a bad king wanted to hurt Jesus. We're going to play a game where we're the wise men. Are you ready?"

Have the children line up behind you. Lead them around the perimeter of the room where it is easy to walk. As you walk, say: "When the wise men traveled to see Baby Jesus, they took the easiest way to get there. Isn't this an easy place to walk?"

Stop. Have the children spread out along one area of the elastic. "Now we're going to be wise men going home a different way. When I tell you to go, step over the elastic or crawl under it. Move carefully, without knocking the elastic down. Ready? Go."

Play the game.

End the game by saying: "As wise men, we traveled through the room in two different ways: around the outside of the room to get there and through the ups and downs in the middle of the room. By going home a different way, the three wise men kept Baby Jesus safe."

85

Bonus Idea

To give children an extra challenge and to teach them opposites, have children move through the elastic in the manner in which you call out. Consider these ideas:

- Over
- Under
- Fast
- Slow
- Backward
- Forward

Ooo! Yuck!
Scripture: Exodus 7-11

This Game Teaches: God sent plagues on the Egyptians when they wouldn't let God's people go.

Supervision Tip: Answer children's questions since some children may wonder why God would send bad things to happen. Focus on the message of following God.

Materials: Three rolls of red crepe paper

Game: Say: "In Bible times, God's people were slaves. The Egyptians wouldn't let them be free, even though God's people asked for freedom over and over. So God's people prayed to God for help, and God sent many different plagues to change the Egyptians' minds (see Exodus 7–11). There were ten different plagues because the Egyptians wouldn't listen to God. So things got worse and worse. We're going to play the games of the ten plagues. Ready?"

Create three groups of children. (They don't have to have the same number of children, just approximately the same.) Clear the play area and have the three groups line up at one end of the room. Give each group one roll of red crepe paper. Say: "When I say go, unroll the crepe paper across the room. Some of you in your group can help unroll while others of you can help hold the end of the crepe paper down so that it creates a long red path." Do the activity. When children finish and get to the other side of the room, say: "The first plague was turning the river to blood. Look at our bloody rivers. Ooo! Yuck!" Teach the children to repeat "Ooo! Yuck!" every time you say it.

Then say: "And things kept getting worse. The bad guy Egyptians still wouldn't free God's people. So then came another plague: Frogs!" Have children hop around like frogs and make frog noises throughout the room. End this part of the game by having the children say "Ooo! Yuck!"

Continue on with the other plagues:

• Gnats and flies—Do these two plagues together by having children flap their arms (like wings), run around the room, and buzz

86

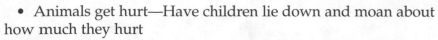

- Animals get hurt—Have children lie down and moan about how much they hurt
- Boils—Have children show all their bruises, scratches, and other owies
- Hail—Have children run around, making crashing sounds like thunder and hail
- Locusts—Have children find a partner and run around together, making buzzing sounds
- Darkness—Shut off the lights and have the children say, "It's dark!"
- People get hurt—Have children find a partner and pretend they're ambulances rushing the hurt people to the hospital. Encourage children to make siren noises as they rush around the room.

End the game by saying: "There were a lot of plagues that came in the Bible. What did you think of that?" Some children will say, "Ooo! Yuck!" Say: "God wants us to listen to God. God's people remained faithful and listened to God."

Jesus Says
Scripture: Luke 5:1-11

This Game Teaches: It's important to follow Jesus and do what Jesus says.

Supervision Tip: Make the game fun, and encourage children to cooperate more by saying "oops" when children move when they're not suppose to.

Materials: None

Game: Ask the children to line up against a wall in the room. Clear the playing area. Ask the children how many have played the game "Simon Says." For those who don't know the game, explain that you're the one who will call out instructions, but this is "Jesus Says," not "Simon Says." Explain that children are to do what you say only if you say "Jesus says" first.

Say things such as these:

• Jesus says follow me by taking two steps (children should do this)

• Jesus says follow me by smiling at another child (children should do this)

• Follow me by shouting "Alleluia!" (children should remain quiet)

• Jesus says follow me by jumping forward three times (children should do this)

• Follow me by taking two small steps (children should not move)

• Follow me by taking two steps backward (children should not move)

• Jesus says follow me by clapping your hands three times (children should do this)

• Jesus says follow me by taking one big step followed by a little step (children should do this)

• Jesus says follow me by shouting "Praise God!" (children should do this)

• Follow me by taking one jump forward (children should not do this)

End the game by saying: "Jesus said a lot of things that are good to do, such as following Jesus. We can learn more about what Jesus said so that we know how to live the Christian life."

Best Friends
Scripture: 1 Samuel 20

This Game Teaches: David and Jonathan were close friends.

Supervision Tip: Monitor how quickly children move around the room so they can have fun and remain safe at the same time.

Materials: Something to play music (a radio, a boom box, or a small stereo)

Game: Make sure there are an even number of children. If not, have an adult join the game. Say: "In the Bible, there were two best friends named David and Jonathan. They loved being together. We're going to play a game about friendship. I'm going to play some music. When you hear the music play, move around the room. You can walk, run, zig zag, move however you wish. As soon as you hear the music stop, grab the hand of someone close to you, raise your hands together in the air and shout 'best friends!' Then keep your hands in the air until everyone has found a partner and done this."

Start playing the music. Encourage children to move around. At some point, stop the music. Encourage children to find a partner, raise their hands together, and shout "best friends" while keeping their hands in the air.

Once everyone has found a partner and raised their hands in the air, say: "We're going to play this again. I will start the music, and I want you to move around the room again. This time, however, find a different partner when the music stops." Play the music and repeat the game. Play the game a few times. (The first few times you play this, the children may need more guidance in how to play. They'll gradually catch on after a few times.)

End the game by saying: "We have a room full of friends. David and Jonathan enjoyed being friends, and it's great to have good friends."

88

Once children learn how to play this game, add another feature to the game. Periodically when you stop the music, yell out, "Everybody is a friend." When children hear that, they are to come together in one large group and do a group hug.

Sinking Peter
Scripture: Mark 6:14-56

This Game Teaches: Jesus helped Peter when he began to sink.

Supervision Tip: Encourage children to watch where they are walking so they don't step on the fingers of crawling children.

Materials: None

Game: Clear a large playing area. Choose one child to be Jesus. Have all the other children line up against one wall. Say: "We're going to play a game of tag, which is different than you're used to. In this game you want to be tagged. Jesus will be the one who does the tagging."

Explain that the children will slowly begin to walk around the room. Tell them that when you say: "Oh! Oh! You're starting to sink," children are to get down on their hands and knees and continue to cross to the other side. Once you've said "Oh! Oh!" the child who is playing Jesus can begin walking around and tagging the crawling children. Once a child has been tagged that child can get up and walk to the other side.

Start the game. Give some guiding instructions if some children aren't following the rules. Typically at this age, children who struggle to follow directions usually aren't being disobedient. They're often confused and need more guidance until they know what they need to do next. Gradually all children will catch on.

Once children get to the other side, choose another child to be Jesus. Repeat the game again.

End the game by saying: "In the Bible, Peter was walking on the water toward Jesus and then he began to sink. Jesus helped Peter so he would be safe." (See Mark 6:14-56.)

89

A Better World
Scripture: Proverbs 3:19-21

This Game Teaches: We can take care of the earth that God created.

Supervision Tip: Encourage children to slow down if they get excited and begin to bump into each other.

Materials: Lots of old newspaper, a wastebasket

Game: Give each child some newspaper. Ask children to tear the newspaper into little pieces and spread the pieces around the room in your designated play area.

Say: "God created our earth, and we can keep it beautiful and clean. Look around at all the newspaper on the floor. We made a big mess, which was a lot of fun, but it's also important that we clean up our messes."

Have the children take off their socks and shoes and place them away from the play area. Say: "Let's clean up the room with our feet and hands!" Demonstrate how to pick up a piece of paper with your toes, then lift your foot to your hand and transfer the paper to your hand. Wad the paper into a ball. Pick up another piece in this way and add the paper to the ball in your hand, making the ball bigger. Have the children try this. Once they catch on, play the game.

End the game when all the newspaper is off the floor. Have children throw their newspaper balls into the wastebasket. Make it a game by placing the wastebasket about a foot away and have them throw the newspaper wads in like basketballs. Say: "God created a wonderful world. We can keep our world clean, just like we cleaned up our room."

90

Love All Around
Scripture: 1 John 4:7-21

This Game Teaches: Love is all around us.

Supervision Tip: Watch children's steps since they may accidentally step on eggs.

Materials: Plastic eggs that open, many small heart stickers, optional: heart-shaped candy

Game: Before the game, place heart stickers (and heart-shaped candy if you wish) inside each plastic egg. Hide the eggs around the playing area, making sure that at least part of the egg is visible.

Bring children together. Say: "Love is all around us, just waiting to be hatched. Look around the room and pick up as many eggs as you can see." Give children time to pick up the eggs. Once they have all the eggs, ask children to sit in a circle. Open the eggs together.

Say: "We're going to take turns around the circle. When it's your turn, peel off your sticker, place it on your shirt and name one person, place, or thing that you love." Start this part of the game. Keep going around the circle until all the eggs are opened and children are covered with stickers.

End the game by saying: "Love is all around us. The Bible says it's good to love one another. Look at your shirts to remember how much love is all around."

91

Higher and Higher
Scripture: Genesis 11:1-9

This Game Teaches: People in the Bible built the tower of Babel.
Supervision Tip: Watch children so they don't trip on spools or try to knock over someone else's tower.
Materials: Lots of thread spools (either with thread or without)
Game: Place all the thread spools on the floor of the playing area. Say: "People in the Bible built a very high tower called the tower of Babel. Let's use these spools and see how big of a tower we can build." If you have more than four children, build more than one tower with about four children working on each tower.

92

Part of the fun of this game is to see how high the tower can be built before it collapses. Once the tower collapses, encourage children to build it again even higher.

End the game by saying: "People building the tower during Bible times had a hard time just like we did. It's always fun, though, to see how high we can build."

Bonus Idea

Wrap boxes of different shapes with wrapping paper, newspaper comic strips, or contact paper. (Some churches wrap boxes in white butcher paper and let the children decorate them with markers and stickers.) Use these wrapped boxes as building blocks for this game—and for other building games and activities.

Glad, Sad, Mad
Scripture: Matthew 5

This Game Teaches: Even though some situations make us sad and mad, it's good to think about what makes us glad.

Supervision Tip: Even though some children may make faces that you'll find humorous, save your laughter for after children leave. Instead, affirm their efforts.

Materials: None

Game: Have children sit in a circle. Demonstrate to children what a mad face looks like. Then have them practice a mad face. Do the same with a sad face and a glad face.

Say: "Some situations make us mad. Others make us sad. Then some make us happy—or glad. I am going to name a situation, and I want you to make the face that matches. Ready?"

Use examples such as these:

- You're mad when someone takes your toy. (Make a mad face.)
- You're sad when someone gets hurt. (Make a sad face.)
- You're glad when someone shares a toy with you. (Make a glad face.)
- You're sad when you see someone cry. (Make a sad face.)
- You're mad when someone kicks another person. (Make a mad face.)
- You're glad when someone wants to play with you. (Make a glad face.)
- You're mad when someone is mean. (Make a mad face.)
- You're sad when you lose a toy. (Make a sad face.)
- You're mad when someone pushes another person. (Make a mad face.)
- You're glad when you make a friend. (Make a glad face.)
- You're sad when you miss your mom or dad. (Make a sad face.)
- You're glad when someone helps you. (Make a glad face.)

End the game by saying: "As human beings, we get mad, sad, and glad at times. The Bible says it's good to be happy and glad."

93

Watch Out, David!
Scripture: 1 Samuel 17

94

This Game Teaches: David protected his sheep from the lion.
Supervision Tip: Watch the child who plays David since some children will try to peek and look even if they don't hear noises.
Materials: None
Game: Ask one child to be David. Choose half of the kids to be sheep and the other half to be lions. Have the child playing David sit on the floor, and have the children who are sheep sit close to him in a cluster. Have the children who are lions line up in another part of the room. Make sure the child playing David has his or her back to where the lions are.

Say: "We're playing a game about David the shepherd. In the Bible, David took care of his sheep and protected them from lions. This wasn't easy to do because lions are very quiet and sneaky. David is going to cover his eyes with his hands and listen closely. So sheep, be very quiet. You want David to listen closely."

Give these instructions to the lions. Say: "Lions, tiptoe quietly toward David and the sheep. If you make a little noise, stop right away. If David doesn't point to you then start tiptoeing toward the sheep. As a lion, you want to tag one sheep before David points to you."

Give one more instruction to David before you play. Say: "David, you have to listen closely. If you hear a noise, keep your eyes covered, turn around and point in the direction of the sound. Don't open your eyes. I will then name the child you are pointing to, and he or she will have to go back to the original line and start over. Ready everybody? Any questions?" Give children time to articulate any questions they have.

Play the game. Name any child David points at and send him or her back to the beginning. If a lion tags a sheep, say "Oh! Oh! A lion got a sheep!" Continue playing.

After awhile, end the game and play again with everybody switching roles.

End the game completely by saying: "David protected his sheep in the Bible from lions. It must have been hard to be a shepherd with all those lions around. But David was a good shepherd."

Play and Laugh
Scripture: Luke 1:46-56

This Game Teaches: Mary was happy about visiting Elizabeth.

Supervision Tip: Have backup balls since they may be bouncing more on the floor than on the tables.

Materials: Table tennis balls, drinking straws, small boxes, masking tape

Game: Set up play areas on tables. Tape a small box to one end of the table and another small box to the other end of the table as goal posts. (If you have more than four children, set up more than one game.)

Give each child a drinking straw. Have one or two children guarding one goal (the small box) and one or two children guarding the other goal. Place a table tennis ball in the middle of the table. Tell the children to try to blow the ball into their opponent's goal with their drinking straw. Give children some time to practice this before they actually play since they may not be familiar with different components of the game. Once they catch on, play.

End the game by saying: "It's fun to play together. Being with others makes us happy. In the Bible, Mary was happy about visiting Elizabeth."

Bonus Idea

To adapt this game for younger children to play, remove the drinking straws. Have young preschoolers blow the ball. (To get balls to really move, have partners blow together.) With older toddlers, let them use their hands to move and stop the ball.

Camel Crawl
Scripture: Genesis 24

This Game Teaches: People rode camels during Bible times.

Supervision Tip: Clear the floor of objects so that children can crawl freely.

Materials: A small pillow (or folded towel) for each child

Game: Stick a small pillow under your shirt in the back. Help insert a pillow under each child's shirt on their backside. Get down on all fours to crawl. Point out how the pillow makes you look like a camel.

Say: "In Bible times, people rode camels to get around. We're going to have a camel crawl." Line up the children at one end of the room. Have them get into a crawling position. Show them where you want them to crawl. Start the game.

When children reach the other side, have them play again, turning around and crawling back to where they first started.

As you play, sing this song to "Twinkle, Twinkle Little Star":

We as camels travel slow
Eating, drinking as we go
Over desert sands we run
In the night and in the sun
We as camels travel slow
Eating, drinking as we go

End the game by saying: "You were a great herd of camels! Just think what it would be like today if we went to church on a camel instead of in a car, a truck, or bus."

96

Bonus Idea

Consider using this also with the scripture of the wise men coming from the East in Matthew 2:1-12. Play the game in the same way but use these lyrics for "Twinkle, Twinkle Little Star":

We as camels travel far
Looking for the great, big star
Up above the world so high
Like a diamond in the sky
We as camels travel far
Looking for the great, big star

A Stormy Sea
Scripture: Luke 8

This Game Teaches: Jesus calms the storm.

Supervision Tip: Encourage children to watch where they are going so they don't bump or poke other children.

Materials: A roll of blue crepe paper streamer and a pair of scissors

Game: Cut a two-foot length of blue crepe paper streamer for each child. Give each child a piece to hold.

Say: "In the Bible, there was a bad storm, which scared a lot of people. When I say the word storm, wave your streamer up and down while you run around the room. When I say be still, stop and sit down while holding your blue crepe paper quietly in your lap."

Play the game. Repeat it a number of times. Later on, ask the children to add sound effects such as using their voices to make thunder sounds and big winds. (Then they can be quiet when they sit.)

End the game by saying: "In the Bible, Jesus calmed a bad storm by telling it to be still. Jesus' words had power that could even stop a bad storm."

97

So Many Animals
Scripture: Genesis 7

98

This Game Teaches: Noah's ark was filled with a variety of animals.

Supervision Tip: Enjoy children's interpretations of their animals while creating an atmosphere of fun.

Materials: Magazine pictures (or simple drawings) of common animals, index cards, tape

Game: Before the game, cut out pictures of different animals from magazines. (Or you can draw simple illustrations or print pictures from the Internet.) Tape one animal on each index card to make a stack of animal cards. (Ideally choose animals that preschoolers recognize, such as farm animals and zoo animals.)

Create a playing area that has a clear starting line and finishing line. Choose one child to be Noah. Have Noah stand in the middle of the playing area. Have the other children line up along the starting area. Give each child an index card with a picture of an animal on it. Tell the children not to show anyone their card or say which animal they have.

Say: "Noah's ark had a lot of animals on it. When you hear the name of your animal, run across the playing area and try to get to the finish line before Noah tags you. If you get caught, stay with Noah and help him catch other animals." Start naming animals and watch them run across the playing area. As soon as you name one animal, name another one so that the game is lively.

Play the game a few times. Have children switch animals and choose a different child to be Noah. Experiment with how quickly or slowly you say animal names.

End the game by saying: "The ark must have been a zoo with all those animals on board. Noah took good care of all the animals and got them to safety after the flood."

Lost Sheep
Scripture: Matthew 18:12-14

This Game Teaches: The shepherd kept looking until the lost sheep was found.

Supervision Tip: Ensure children are gentle when seeking out the sheep since some children can become overly excited and accidentally play rough.

Materials: None

Game: Choose one child to be the sheep. Have another adult take the children out of the room and give them instructions in the hallway. That adult can say something like: "When it is time, we will go in the room. Start looking around the room for the lost sheep. Besides looking carefully also listen carefully since the sheep will sometimes baa."

While the group of children are in the hallway, tell the child designated to be the sheep to hide somewhere in the room. Help the child if you wish. Ideally, you want the child to be well hidden. Say: "Everyone will soon come into the room to look for you. Be very quiet and very still. I will sing a song. When I stop, baa two times."

Invite the children into the room. As they look for the lost sheep, sing this song to the tune of "Oh Where, Oh Where Has My Little Dog Gone?"

Oh where, oh where has my little sheep gone
Oh where, oh where can it be?
With its cute little ears and its white, fuzzy wool
Oh where, oh where can it be?

Pause. If the child doesn't baa, invite the child to do so. Play until the sheep is found. Then repeat with another child being the sheep (or having two or three children acting as sheep at the same time if you have a large group).

End the game by saying: "The Bible tells a story about a sheep getting lost and how the shepherd looked and looked until he found the sheep."

99

A Long Laugh
Scripture: Psalm 68:3-4

This Game Teaches: It's great to be happy and giggle for joy.

Supervision Tip: Model different laughs and giggles for children, which often can invite even more laughter.

Materials: A feather or handkerchief

Game: Have children spread out across the room facing you. Say: "We're going to play a laughing game. When I throw this feather (or handkerchief) in the air, start laughing as loudly as you can. As soon as the feather (or handkerchief) hits the floor, stop right away and do not laugh."

Play the game. Most children will have a hard time stopping when they're suppose to, which often can start more laughing fits. Do this a number of times and really cut loose. Try some outrageous laughs yourself and see what happens. (The whole point of the game is to laugh and have outrageous fun.)

End the game by saying: "The Bible says it's great to be happy and laugh. It's so much fun to laugh. I love to laugh with you, and God loves it when we laugh."

100

Follow Christ the Leader
Scripture: Mark 1:16-20

This Game Teaches: It's important to follow Christ.

Supervision Tip: Encourage children to go slowly so they don't slip or trip.

Materials: Lots of wooden blocks (or another type of block that is sturdy enough to step on)

Game: Scatter blocks on the floor in the playing area of your room. Ask for a volunteer to be Jesus Christ, who is the leader. Have the rest of the children line up behind your leader.

Say: "In the Bible, Jesus said to follow him. We're going to play a game of follow the Jesus leader. Jesus raise your hand." Ask the child to raise his or her hand. Say: "Now our leader will take us walking through this area. Watch closely since the leader may step on some blocks and around some others. Follow the leader the best that you can."

Play the game. Recognize that children in the back may not be able to see as well and will not be able to follow the leader as well as the children in front. That's okay. The point is for the children to follow the leader the best they can.

After one or two minutes, stop the game. Ask for another volunteer to be the leader. Repeat the game again.

End the game by saying: "The disciples in the Bible followed Jesus when Jesus asked them to follow him. Today, Jesus still asks us to follow him, and I'm glad when we do."

101

Bonus Idea

Consider setting up the blocks in a pattern that has different paths, such as in a circle with an X in it. Children can step only on the blocks and take different routes, such as around the circle and then through the circle and then partially around the circle again before going through the other part of the circle.

The Best Bibles for Young Children

E ven though young children cannot read the Bible, it's essential that they begin to recognize that one book (the Bible) contains stories of faith. Whenever you're working with young children (whether you're in a nursery or a classroom), have a number of picture Bibles around for children to look at and for adults to read from. Countless picture Bibles are now published. The following is a list of a few that work well with different age groups.

Bibles for Infants

- *Baby's Bible Friends: Playtime Book* by Simone Abel (Cincinnati: Standard Publishing, 2000). This eight-page cloth book includes two stuffed animals (a lamb and a bear) and emphasizes the animals in the Bible, which babies love.

- *Baby's First Bible* by Pd (Pleasantville, N.Y.: Reader's Digest Books, 1996). This twenty-page board book with a handle and peek-through windows focuses on ten classic Bible stories.

- *Baby's First Bible* by Standard Publishing (Cincinnati: Standard Publishing, 1996). This Bible features scripture verses, rhymes, and die-cut windows.

Bibles for Toddlers

- *God Loves Me Bible* by Susan Elizabeth Beck (Grand Rapids, Mich.: Zondervan, 1993). Each Bible story in this 168-page book is illustrated with colorful art.

- *The Toddler's Bible* by V. Gilbert Beers (Colorado Springs: Chariot Victor Books, 1992). The 125 simple Bible stories with 400 illustrations was developed especially for toddlers.

- *The Bible in Pictures for Toddlers* by Ella K. Lindvall (Chicago: Moody Press, 2003). Written by a former elementary school teacher, this Bible includes seventy Bible stories from the Old and New Testaments.

Bibles for Young Preschoolers

- *My First Bible in Pictures* by Kenneth N. Taylor (Carol Stream, Ill.: Tyndale House, 2004). Each Bible story is simplified to one page with a colorful illustration. The book includes a handle for easy carrying and a total of 125 Bible stories from the Old and New Testaments.

- *Early Readers Bible* by V. Gilbert Beers (Grand Rapids, Mich.: Zondervan, 2001). Children will discover sixty-four easy-to-read Bible stories. The author wrote this book using the standard public school list of words for beginning readers.

Bibles for Older Preschoolers

- *Children's Illustrated Bible* by Selina Hastings (London: DK Publishing, 1994). This Bible combines the thoughtful work of biblical scholars and is written and designed to appeal to children. Maps, colorful photographs, and illustrations make this Bible as interesting to look at as to read.

- *Little Kids Adventure Bible* by Larry Richards and Lawrence O. Richards (Grand Rapids, Mich.: Zondervan, 2000). This 448-page Bible is ideal for older preschoolers since it includes Bible stories written for short attention spans but also illustrates the depth of the Bible.

- *The Children's Bible Story Book* by Anne de Graaf (Nashville: Thomas Nelson, 1991). This 308-page Bible is packed with three hundred stories from the Bible.

Bibles for Young African American Children

- *Holy Bible: Illustrated Especially for Children of Color* by World Bible Publishing (Iowa Falls: World Bible Publishing, 1998). This Bible (in the New International Version) includes illustrated portraits of African American men and women.

- *Children of Color Storybook Bible* by Victor Hogan (Nashville: Nelson Bibles, 2001). This book combines rich art work depicting African Americans and the Contemporary English Version of the Bible.

Bibles for Young Spanish-Speaking Children

- *Mi Primera Biblia En Cuadros* by Ken Taylor (Miami: Spanish House, 1996). This book is the Spanish translation of *My First Bible in Pictures* by Kenneth N. Taylor.

- *La Biblia Para Ninos* by Usborne Books (London: Usborne, 2000). This Bible includes rich illustrations accompanied by Spanish text for four- to eight-year-olds.

- *Mi Primera Biblia Ilustrada* by E. Reeves (Miami: Spanish House, 1999). This 128-page Bible includes many colorful illustrations for young children.

The Best Resources on Early Childhood Development

A plethora of resources exist on early childhood development. Some are more academic in nature, while many are a bit too simplistic. For congregational leaders, volunteers, and parents looking for practical resources based on sound developmental theory and research, here are some of the best resources around.

Resources on Childhood Spiritual Development

- *Real Kids, Real Faith: Practices for Nurturing Children's Spiritual Lives* by Karen Marie Yust (San Francisco: Jossey-Bass, 2004). This groundbreaking book focuses on practical ways to foster children's spiritual and religious lives from birth to age twelve.

- *Stages of Faith: The Psychology of Human Development and the Quest for Meaning* by James W. Fowler (San Francisco: HarperSanFrancisco, 1981). For anyone interested in the stages of faith that a person goes through (from infancy through adulthood), this book highlights what happens in the context of overall human development.

Resources on Infant Development

- *The First Three Years of Life: New and Revised* by Burton L. White (New York: Prentice Hall Press, 1985). This classic book explores in detail the way babies grow and develop.

- *Caring for Your Baby and Young Child: Birth to Age 5*, edited by Steven P. Shelov, M.D. (New York: Bantam, 1991). Chapters 6 through 9 focus on the rapid changes babies go through during their first year of life.

Resources on Toddler Development

- *Your One-Year-Old: The Fun-Loving, Fussy 12- to 24-Month-Old* by Louise Bates Ames, Frances Ilg, and Carol Chase Haber (New York: Dell, 1982). This easy-to-use book is based on research and includes ideas on how to respond when toddlers act out.

- *Your Two-Year-Old: Terrible or Tender* by Louise Bates Ames and Frances Ilg (New York: Dell, 1976). Focusing only on how two-year-olds develop into three-year-olds, this valuable book gives adults insights into how to play and interact with toddlers.

- *Caring for Your Baby and Young Child: Birth to Age 5*, edited by Steven P. Shelov, M.D. (New York: Bantam, 1991). Chapters 10 and 11 feature the physical, language, cognitive, social, and emotional milestones of toddlers.

- *The First Three Years of Life: New and Revised* by Burton L. White (New York: Prentice Hall Press, 1985). Wonder why toddlers do what they do? This book explains why and gives suggestions on how to respond most effectively.

Resources on Preschool Development

- *Your Three-Year-Old: Friend or Enemy* by Louise Bates Ames and Frances Ilg (New York: Dell, 1985). Why does a three-year-old seem to be friendly one moment and then turn on you? This book tells why and gives suggestions on how to deal with a wide range of behaviors.

- *Your Four-Year-Old: Wild and Wonderful* by Louise Bates Ames and Frances Ilg (New York: Dell, 1976). This book captures the essence of four-year-olds and how to bring out the best in them.

- *Your Five-Year-Old: Sunny and Serene* by Louise Bates Ames and Frances Ilg (New York: Dell, 1979). A delightful age, this book explores why so many adults enjoy this age group and describes how to play and talk with them.

- *Caring for Your Baby and Young Child: Birth to Age 5*, edited by Steven P. Shelov, M.D. (New York: Bantam, 1991). Chapter 12 outlines the changes preschoolers go through as they grow from age three to age five.

Scripture Index

Topical Index